walkin' the talk

walkin' the talk

Keepin' the Faith in Africentric Congregations

Julia M. Speller

THE PILGRIM PRESS
CLEVELAND

DEDICATION

To my parents,

Quinville Allen and Nellie P. Harris-Allen.

The Pilgrim Press, 700 Prospect Avenue, Cleveland, Ohio 44115-1100, thepilgrimpress.com

© 2005 by Julia M. Speller

Scripture quotations, unless otherwise noted, are from the New Revised Standard Version of the Bible, © 1989 by the Division of Christian Education of the National Council of Churches of Christ in the United States of America and are used by permission. Changes have been made for inclusivity.

Printed in the United States of America on acid-free paper

09   08   07   06   05   5   4   3   2   1

Library of Congress Cataloging-in-Publication Data

Speller, Julia M., 1951–
    Walkin' the talk : keepin' the faith in africentric congregations /
Julia M. Speller.
        p. cm.
    Includes bibliographical references (p.   ) and index.
    ISBN 0-8298-1522-8 (alk. paper)
        1. African American churches.   2. African Americans—Religion.
3. Afrocentrism—Religious aspects—Christianity.   I. Title.

BR563.N4S65   2005
277.3'083'08996073—dc22

2005022479

contents

CONTENTS

Foreword

THE RELIGIOUS EXPERIENCE OF AFRICAN AMERICANS has never been monolithic. While the term "the black religious experience" implies the presence of homogeneous congregations whose worship experiences, theologies, spiritualities, and forms of ministry mirror each other, this is far from the truth. Since 1619, persons of African descent in America have worshiped in bush arbors and camp meetings; they have formed congregations within independent black denominations and have joined congregations in mainline white denominations. They have also founded communities of faith with radical notions of identity and nationalism both inside and outside of Christianity. Together this suggests distinctive religious experiences, theologies, spiritualities, and ministry that dissolve naive notions of religious homogeneity and sameness. In this book, Julia Speller takes us on a tour that reveals yet another layer of this congregational diversity, through the contemporary expression of "an Africentric spirituality."

She proposes that a historic dialectic of oppositions among African American traditions and all others is not a problem to overcome but a cause to celebrate, as we discover alternative visions of hope, meaningful expressions of faith, and practical proposals for living our lives in community. She is aware that there are a number of critics of Africentric spirituality. Some reject it as un-Christian and others interpret it as a passing trend. Still others see it as a form of religious syncretism that must be shunned. Syncretism. This loaded term is used to distinguish between the pure religion of Christianity and other less pure adulterated forms that emerge from it, but this is clearly not what the author intends to show. She agrees, instead, with Catherine Albanese, who, in her book *American Religions and Religion,* prefers the term "combinationism," which honors and celebrates religious innovation through culturally in-spired traditions, worship, and practice. It is from this perspective that the author views Africentric congregations and their emergent spirituality as a valuable contribution to the diversity of the "black religious experi-ence" and the American religious landscape as well.

On this tour of Africentric congregations, Dr. Speller shows herself to be an adept theorist, in two senses of the term. First, the very word comes from *theoria,* the Greek term that means to behold, to look at. She is a gifted guide who helps the reader look, and to look discern-ingly, to notice what might otherwise be overlooked. At the same time, she is a theorist in the conventional sense in that she brings theory to bear on her observations and then helps us readers to do our own the-orizing. Oh yes, she is also practical-minded, as the last chapter shows, when, after the tour, she takes pains to prevent us from being voyeurs, eavesdroppers, kibitzers, hitchhikers. She wants readers to use their imaginations and summon courage to give expression to such fusions of faith and culture.

Dr. Speller is particularly familiar with contemporary literature de-voted to studying what makes up a congregation and what might make it function well. She has read her sociology, studied ethnography, and re-veals at-homeness with various "-ologies" and "-graphies" that become tools for clarifying, not guises that obscure. To achieve her goals, the au-thor must be and is bold, courageous about defining, defending without defensiveness, showing emotional range all the way over to disappoint-ment and frustration without ever letting them turn her to anger. As a tour leader, she invites us along with her, as a theorist she makes us think, as a practitioner she tutors us.

Her take on the key work, "spirituality," is fresh and vital. She knows that the very term can signal individualized seeking, even self-centered searching. It is, however, too creative a concept to be jettisoned by those who seek community and would turn worship and education and the common life into service of others. We have heard spirituality defined thus: after you have taken out everything you don't like in "religion," what is left is spirituality—but not in this strong book. Dr. Speller is not afraid of "religion," if religion also includes communal expression, congregational life, and practical living.

What we look for in a guide, whether on a walk in nature or a tour of a city, is someone who both notices what we might not and then interprets what we see. The Imani Temple Christian Fellowship, First Afrikan Presbyterian Church, and Trinity United Church of Christ, objects of suspicion to many African Americans and perhaps more whites, deserve the careful, close-up look Dr. Speller provides. She is not content only to point her finger, her camera, her paragraphs, and our attention at places and practices that looked alienating and exotic at first glance. Stay around, she beckons, and you are likely to learn from all, as you come to feel at home in them.

Julia Speller does not suggest that these three places and programs are exhaustive; they are samples, representative, out of many possibilities. Paying attention to what they embody and what she reveals, however, can inform and help equip anyone who wants to express Africentric spirituality or to understand it better. I can even picture that the implied lessons and the practical approach at the end of the book could be of use to Christians who, by analogy, want to experiment with "Asian" or "Hispanic" or "Native American" centricity as they form or express community. As a matter of fact, those who lead or participate in largely "European" derived or "white" Christianity might find that her examples can serve as mirrors held up for them better to see themselves and their "combinationism" or as windows on worlds in which they might better witness and serve. In other words, this is a book for all sorts of Christians or onlookers who know how rich the potential of their congregations can be in the human city, where they pursue the common good.

Martin E. Marty
Fairfax M. Cone Distinguished Service Professor Emeritus
The University of Chicago

Preface

IN HER BOOK OF SHORT STORIES *In Love and Trouble: Stories of Black Women,* Alice Walker tells a poignant story entitled "Diary of an African Nun." In it she gives a glimpse of the intimate thoughts of a young nun who lives and teaches in her Ugandan village. The nun proudly described herself as the wife of Christ who was born in a village "civilized" by American missionaries. But in her room at night, she listened to the chants and felt the rhythms of the drums in the village and lamented the war waging within her as she said,

> My mouth must be silent, then, though my heart jumps to the booming of the drums as the last strong pulse of life in a dying world. . . . To assure life for my people in this world I must be among the lying ones and teach them to die. I will turn their dances into prayers to an empty sky . . ."[1]

She understood that the Christian commitment that she embraced was one that denied the "booming of the drums" and the urge to dance for the sake of an "empty sky." For this nun, acceptance of Christianity presupposed the relinquishing of her Africanness—a thankless task that she believed must be taught to her people for life in this world and the next. This conscious decision to separate her Africanness from her Christianity was, paradoxically, a living death because it cut deep, dividing her faith from her culture.

The dilemma of this African nun has a haunting familiarity for me as a teen who, during the 1960s, experienced "desegregation" in northern schools. As one of less than a hundred students who integrated a public high school in Chicago, chants of "Black Power" held for me the same passion as the "booming drums" did for her. It also promised alienation for me from the white majority in my new environment if I heeded the call. My adolescent desire to fit in and be liked led to varying levels of assimilation for sheer survival. This paralleled the nun's decision to ignore the drums and to choose what seemed to be the safest way, though it was admittedly a silent death. I also remember so clearly my feelings of guilt about not courageously embracing my identity like some of my sisters and brothers just as the nun felt ashamed of her selected barrenness in a village where she was surrounded by children.

Many African American congregations, particularly since the 1960s, have also struggled with what seemed to be a contradiction in their identity. Some have done what they could to fit into the mold of their white mainline denominations, much like I did in my high school. Others, like the nun, have chosen silence. They muffled the potentially healing rhythms of Africa within the collective memory of their congregations in favor of a life and ministry disconnected from their God-given identity as African and their God-inspired identity as Christian. In my own experience, I found wholeness when I decided to view my identity holistically, striking a creative and complementary balance between all its parts. What was most helpful for me was to begin with who I am as a daughter of Africa living in America. Once I was able to truly embrace that reality of birth, my faith commitment as a Christian took on new meaning. I heard the gospel message as a promise of liberation *from* eternal death in the world to come but also a promise of liberation *for* works of justice in this world. A growing number of contemporary African American congregations are doing the same thing as they bring together their culture and faith traditions and, as a result, their ministries reflect a vibrancy that heals, restores, and transforms.

The main focus of this book, therefore, is to profile a representative sample of these faith communities who have adopted a both/and rather than an either/or posture in balancing their culture and faith. In their ministries, they simultaneously hear, acknowledge, and walk to the rhythm of the drums within but also talk through their congregational life and mission in the words of a liberating gospel that brings life, healing, and empowerment. This book will, consequently, profile congregations that have found ways to ignite congregational vitality and sharpen Christian witness through an Africentric spirituality. It is my hope that this book will guide African American congregations into their own interpretations of and responses to what it means to combine faith and cultural identity so that their walk and talk will be authentically their own, while sharing, celebrating, and living the promise of Christ's gospel of liberation.

Acknowledgments

WHILE RESEARCH AND WRITING ARE SOLITARY ENDEAVORS, the creation of a book requires aid and support from a variety of sources to be successful. I have been blessed to receive encouragement, critique, and help from a variety of sources, to whom I am eternally grateful. My initial idea regarding this topic was not to write a book, but rather a study guide to help African American congregations explore religious practices. Through a grant from the Valparaiso Project on Education and Formation and the encouragement of Dorothy Bass and Don Richter, I was able to gather a gifted group of consultants that included Karen Hutt, Reginald Blount, Eddie Knox, Jerry D. Blakemore, Jeffrey P. Radford, Darrell George Mayfield, Emily Hooper-Lansana, and Sharon Mitchell. Through their wise counsel, my horizons were broadened, and it became apparent that a book needed to be written on the topic.

Chicago Theological Seminary, as the institution that supports and affirms my professional work and development, offers and encourages an early sabbatical leave for junior faculty after only several semesters of full-time teaching. It was during this time that I was able to step out of the rigor of designing, preparing, and teaching initial courses to explore areas of intellectual curiosity. Without this time, the book would have taken many more years. Martin E. Marty, the chair of my doctoral committee, added another vital layer of support to my professional development. During my early days of research, he challenged me to think in broader contexts using my own distinctive lens. I am grateful for his continuing support evidenced in his willingness to provide the foreword for this book. Additional financial support during two summers came from Louisville Institute and Wabash Center for Teaching and Learning. These sources provided excellent insights through Jim Lewis and Paul Myhre into how to prepare grant proposals and evaluate research content and methodology, which are invaluable skills that will help me as I continue in my professional career.

This kind of research could never take place without the hospitality and trust of committed congregations, to whom I extend my heartfelt gratitude. Imani Temple Christian Fellowship and First Afrikan Presbyterian Church both welcomed me as one of their own, making the participant-observer experience very rewarding. Pastors Jelani F. Kafela and Mark A. Lomax became colleagues as well as brothers as we shared the hopes and dreams as well as the challenges and fears of what it really means to claim and live a gospel of liberation from an Africentric perspective. Trinity United Church of Christ continued to be both my nurturing nest as well as my launching pad for my ongoing ministry. Here, participant-observer posture was experienced at a more intimate level as I relived many historic moments in the life of this community of faith. Pastor Jeremiah A. Wright Jr. has from the beginning affirmed and acknowledged my call as a layperson, respecting it on the same level as those who are "officially" ordained. He has never failed to be my teacher, mentor, brother, and friend throughout the past thirty-two years, and I extend my heartfelt thanks.

Efficient and effective technical assistance is a must in any research endeavor; I am indebted to several who rose to the occasion. Jacqueline Trussell and Tolonda Henderson were able research assistants who tackled the tedium of library work, while Vivian Rios spent long hours transcribing interview tapes. Janeea L. Speller, my daughter, provided clerical assistance for the Valparaiso Project and later helped me fine-tune the bibliography. But more importantly, she endured my anxious moments with patience and love as the project approached completion. Together, those named created a web of technical support that was dedicated to detail through their diverse skills. Another level of technical expertise was made available through three readers who each brought a different lens. Don Richter gave a greater appreciation for religious/ spiritual practices in congregational life, Iva E. Carruthers encouraged deeper thought on the realities of race and ethnicity and the need to affirm an African identity in America, and Daphne Wiggins brought insights in method and analysis within a congregational context. Together they stretched me to explore this project from a variety of angles and to ask different and more profound questions.

Finally, there was ongoing and continuous support from family and friends. My husband and partner in life for the past thirty-four years, Clyde E. Speller Jr., knows me so well that he was able to discern when I needed space and when I needed to be rescued from my own compulsive nature. I thank God for his strong and persistent presence in my life. My sisters, Verdi P. Allen-Thomas and Cora I. Allen-Brown, along with so many other family and friends, continued to ask the question, "Is it done yet?" While often annoying, this query reminded me that I was not alone in this process and that the thoughts and prayers of others were with me. While my other daughter, Chrishawn A. Speller, and my son, Clyde A. Speller, live miles away from me, their support and affirmation was always a source of encouragement. Their sentiments are shared by my father, Quinville Allen, who with my late mother, Nellie P. Harris-Allen, demonstrated many years ago what real commitment looks like in a congregational context. They were the ones who actually modeled a life of practiced spirituality as they taught my sisters and I, through word and deed, how to walk the talk and keep the faith.

And finally, thanks to the ancestors upon whose shoulders I stand. To God be the glory!

Introduction

RELIGIOUS CONGREGATIONS ARE AMONG the most resilient institutions in American society and they are the primary communities where faith is expressed and perpetuated.[1] They are understood as subcultures within a larger culture that have distinct, "thick" identities made up of complex networks of meaning. They define and transmit values, establish and regulate patterns of behavior, and identify and create artifacts.[2] Congregations are held together by much more than creeds, polity, and programs. Each one has an internal language or idiom[3] found in their stories, symbols, rituals, and values. Since the early twentieth century, congregations have been the subject of inquiry for Protestant ministers looking for more effective ways to provide ministry in America's growing urban centers. This need led to a number of "descriptive sociological inquiries," creating a sociology of congregations.[4] As time passed, scholars employed ethnographic as well as social-science approaches as they studied congregations. More recently, historians entered the picture, seeking to highlight the complexities of congregational life using narrative lenses that looked at the past and the present at once, as they anticipated the future. One fine example of the use of congregational studies is found in the two-volume work of James W. Lewis and James P. Wind, *American Congregations*. Volume 1 profiles twelve diverse American congregations while volume 2 critically discusses the selected issues and implications of these stories. Together they provide what Lewis and Wind describe as a "much needed corrective [to the] static images" of congregations from ethnographic and sociological inquiry alone.[5]

Of the variety of methods used to explore congregational culture, a focus on storytelling as a research tool, says sociologist of religion, Wade Clark Roof, is worthy of consideration. He views storytelling in a congregational setting as a vital part of the narrative tradition that "affirms who we are and gives identity, purpose, and meaning to our existence."[6] Embedded in these narratives, he continues, is the "power to sharpen our sensitivities to virtue and truth." The stories found in congregations, both individual and corporate, are rich reservoirs of meaning that reveal "the nuances and shades of subtleties"[7] found as a people of God attempt to walk the talk and keep the faith.

This is no less the case in African American congregations. Historically the church has been and remains the strongest and most enduring institution in black communities as well as the keeper of the sacred stories of African peoples who have embraced Christianity in America. Beginning nearly four hundred years ago, African slaves gathered overtly and covertly in congregations that helped define meaning and establish a sense of belonging in a world that limited their potential and discounted their humanity. Through a strong oral tradition reminiscent of the Djoli (storyteller)[8] of West Africa, these women and men kept the tradition alive by using stories, sermons, folk-wisdom, and songs that creatively merged the sacred and the secular aspects of life into one experience. As the "safest place on earth," the local congregation became an alternative culture[9] that nurtured hope as African Americans reflected on the biblical stories of the Israelites and were encouraged along their own journeys. Undergirding this rich narrative culture was an abiding spirituality, born on the continent of Africa, shaped in the brush arbors of southern plantations in America, and matured in the midst of congregational life. It is a spirituality that understands the gospel message as one that speaks of liberation from sin and death but also liberation for life and service. It is also a spirituality that connects the stories of the African past with the realities of an American present in ways that empower its people to walk the talk and keep the faith in the days to come.

This Africentric spirituality is essentially one response to what it means to be black and Christian in America. In his book *Africentric Christianity: A Theological Appraisal for Ministry,* J. Deotis Roberts acknowledges the historic tension experienced by Africans in Diaspora of living in exile and the need to have a place of center to call home.[10] Acknowledging the use of the Exodus paradigm by black and liberationist theologians and the Hagar paradigm by womanist theologians,[11] he suggests movement to a new way of doing theology from an Africentric perspective.

> The groundwork for this powerful redemptive theology is clearly before us. It is a place where our experience and the biblical record meet. The Exile experience is as real to us as the Exodus.[12]

This emphasis on exile and acknowledgment of an African Diaspora was also referenced by Theophus H. Smith in 1989 in an essay entitled "The Spirituality of Afro-American Traditions."[13] In it he noted the insights of African American theologian Charles Shelby Rooks, who proposed "a possible new image of an African Diaspora based on the Biblical story of the Babylonian Exile and the final Jewish Diaspora. It is to the end of the biblical history of Israel that Black America must look rather than to the beginning."[14] Smith affirms Rooks's focus on the power of the biblical narrative and suggests important "religious-ethical or spiritual implications" in the diasporal motif. He concludes that it points to a transcendent dimension that becomes an important interpretative tool for communities that claim a strong biblical self-identification.[15]

As with their sisters and brothers in other parts of the Diaspora, African captives in America had to negotiate what it meant to be persons of faith who were separated from their cultural home. The result of this struggle was a distinctive and complex connection with the Divine, lived out in the context of human communality. African exiles in Cuba, Brazil, and Haiti, for example, gave birth to Santeria, Candomble, and Vodou, respectively, as they sought and found meaning; likewise, African slaves in America created comparable spiritual expressions. They began with slave religion and expressions of evangelical Protestantism in the eighteenth and nineteenth centuries. During this time there was a diversity of experiences as some claimed membership in mainline white denominations but many more established congregations within independent black denominations. There were more distinctive religious experiences like the United Negro Improvement Association and the Nation of Islam in the twentieth century, yet over time an underlying spirituality was present that pointed to Africa in varying degrees as a cultural home that provided meaning for each historical time. Africentric[16] spirituality in contemporary African American congregations, consequently, is not a mirror reflection of African spiritualities on the continent but is yet another reinterpretation and reappropriation through backward glance while stepping forward in the midst of exile.[17]

In his discussion on Africentric Christianity, Roberts acknowledges Kwanzaa and Christmas as "powerful symbols of the tension between Africentricity and Christianity . . . as two perspectives of black life, one cultural and one religious."[18] He cautions, however, against allowing the former to replace the latter. While I agree with his basic position, I believe that the use of the word "centrism" to describe both faith and culture is problematic and prevents the harmony he seeks. I use instead the terms "centeredness" and "rootedness" to locate culture and faith respectively. This gives room for a harmony that becomes a part of the framework for an Africentric spirituality in the spirit of a both/and way of thinking.

With this in mind, I identify the growing number of congregations that explicitly attempt to bring together faith and culture as Christ-rooted and African-centered. The former is the faith commitment where African American Christians find redemption, while the latter is the social and cultural location where they live their lives. This position is, therefore, not an attempt to replace African-centeredness with Christ-centeredness. It is an effort to bring creative harmony between the two by embracing the authority found in the rooting foundation of the Christian tradition and by acknowledging the cultural reality of daily living.

It is with this as the backdrop that I argue that there is a distinctive experience of spirituality in contemporary Africentric congregations. They tap into the richness of an African spiritual worldview, reshaping and reinterpreting it into an experience that is culturally relevant for them in the American religious context. In their worship and ministries, Christ-rooted and African-centered congregations display cultural pride through artifacts, rituals, music, and dance, and they have an active knowledge of and appreciation for the history and culture of African peoples from antiquity to the present. It is important to note, however, that their Africentric identity is not based solely on the things they do or the knowledge they have acquired but on their self-identity as a part of a larger African Diaspora, revealing an important notion of communality. This shows a distinctive psychological shift that makes what they wear, how they worship and adorn their sanctuaries, and the history they recite only secondary to their self-understanding as African people. Ultimately, their understanding of self and community does not begin and end with their culture. These Africentric congregations have learned to view their Christian commitment through cultural lenses yielding a both/and understanding of who they are that harmoniously combines sacred and secular, faith and culture.

One of the sources that many of them use to inform their spirituality is the Nguzo Saba or the Seven Principles of Kwanzaa. These principles celebrate Africentric values in an annual ritual, and many congregations align them liturgically with Christmas,[19] but they also have the potential to further inform their mission and ministry in daily life.[20] This effort to acknowledge and capitalize on the valuable impact of these principles is not restricted to a congregational context but one that is shared across academic disciplines as well. Over the past two decades, for example, practitioners and researchers in the social sciences have recognized the inadequacy of some of their theoretical and conceptual frameworks. This is particularly noted when applied in the assessment and analysis of issues that confront the African American family and community. Many, consequently, have identified and used the Nguzo Saba as a useful tool for "assessing the damage enslavement, racism, and capitalism have caused the [African American] family" and helping . . . "resurrect, reclaim, and create African Culture and the African personality."[21] In a similar manner, I will use the Nguzo Saba as interpretive lenses to discuss living examples of Africentric spirituality seen in selected congregations, with the expressed purpose of identifying ways to expand their use beyond the annual celebrations.

It is important to acknowledge that Africentricity as an intellectual movement is not without its critics. In the minds of many scholars, black and white, it is seen as reverse racist, antiwhite, culturally chauvinistic, and separatist.[22] Even in local churches, many firmly believe that an emphasis on an Africentric identity is in diametric opposition to an affirmation that upholds an identity in Christ. In an ideal world this would be true. Unfortunately, in light of the continuing struggles of being black in America, there is a need to regain and maintain a positive sense of self and experience a heightened level of individual and communal wholeness that prepares African Americans for engagement in the world as subjects and not objects. Through Africentric lenses, the mandates and commitments of the Christian gospel take on new dimensions. The liberation of African peoples all over the world, for example, ceases to be an exclusive, ethnically centered goal when seen through Africentric lenses that honor and respect the totality of humanity as a divine expression of God.

Iva Carruthers speaks to this point in her master's thesis, "For Such a Time as This: A Pan African Theopraxis." In it she introduces the concept of Pan African Theopraxis as "the sacred activity of discerning and effecting God-talk and action in African and oppressed communities of the world [with] action and ethics as its core." She points to this approach as a challenge to "all Christians and other peoples of God." Hence, Africentricity in a congregational context, like Pan African Theopraxis in the global context, ideally points to a solidarity that is centered on culture and finds its fullest expression when it is grounded in a divine imperative and moves toward liberation of all humankind.[23]

The intent of this study is not to romanticize African heritage or to idealize Africentric congregations, for there are a growing number of black churches across the country that provide phenomenal ministries without explicit emphasis on African heritage and culture. This book, however, is an attempt to highlight a phenomenon that has emerged more explicitly in the past fifteen to twenty years. It is an effort to open up a new chapter in the religious history and culture of Americans generally and African Americans more specifically. I believe that there was a subtle but important shift that occurred during the late 1980s and '90s that moved some culturally aware black congregations toward a more ontologically based African-centeredness in the same way that many churches moved from "Negro" to "black" in the cultural renaissance of the 1960s. The major reason for this earlier shift, identified by C. Eric Lincoln,[24] was the heightened level of self-consciousness that resulted from the struggles for civil rights, the subsequent emergence of the Black Power movement, and the birth of black theology. I believe that this more recent shift in consciousness is not simply a nostalgic remnant of the 1970s or a resurgence of the black nationalism of that era but is evidence of a continuing evolution in consciousness that moved many congregations toward a more explicit expression of Africentricity.

This shift of consciousness did not occur in a vacuum but came forth as a result of intellectual, political, and social realities of the time. In the field of education, for example, Molefe Asante's books, articles, and essays on the concept of "Afrocentricity" during the 1980s and 1990s[25] pushed scholars to debate the need for an alternative perspective to the prevailing European ideology. This created space for the peoples of African descent to be "at the center of any analysis that involves African culture and behavior,"[26] and has also greatly influenced debates on the value of multiculturalism in schools and other organizations and institutions.[27]

It was also during this time that social theorists and epistemologists (those who study the nature of knowledge) made a "postmodern turn" that challenged the power of "metanarratives" that made sweeping generalizations about human experience that left many at the margins of a white, male universe.[28] For some American religious scholars, the traditionally held white Anglo-Saxon Protestant orientation that marginalizes and systematically silences many voices is henceforth unacceptable. In a similar frame, many black feminists refocused away from their primary identity as women to the more particular concerns of women of color. In so doing, they gave birth to the womanist movement, which spoke more accurately and meaningfully to their issues of race, class, and gender.[29] Using the disciplines of ethics, theology, and biblical studies, they take old religious language and symbols and give them new meaning through a more holistic methodology and worldview.[30] The sentiments that fueled these intellectual movements of the 1980s by decentering and recentering discussion on human life and experience became the impetus for many culturally conscious congregations of the time to begin a move from being black to being African.

During these same years, political issues on the continent of Africa took a more prominent place in the consciousness of America. In South Africa, for example the anti-apartheid protests were acknowledged internationally with the divestment of millions of dollars from South Africa by religious and social institutions. The liberation of Nelson Mandela in 1991, his election as president of South Africa in 1994, and the subsequent dismantling of apartheid created a new connection across the African Diaspora. In the midst of an ever-shrinking global village, these and other continental events made the peoples, cultures, and issues of Africa more tangible. They give the term "African Diaspora" new meaning for many African Americans. Within culturally conscious congregations, mission dollars given to faraway African peoples took on a more personal reality as they began to identify more intimately with the struggles and hopes of their sisters and brothers on the African continent. Many congregations began to travel to parts of Africa with less of a mind for tourism and shopping and more of a mind for pilgrimage. Many of these trips resulted in personal awakenings that recognized biological as well as spiritual connections to the land and peoples of Africa.

By the early 1990s, intellectual discussions about "Afrocentricity," political events in Africa, and congregational experiences of traveling to Africa added excitement to congregations seeking to effectively combine African culture and Christian faith. Another important trend in black congregational life during that time, however, came as a result of a growing middle class and shifting demographics of the early 1990s. Anthony B. Pinn in his book *The Black Church in the Post–Civil Rights Era* points out that, following the struggles of the 1960s, economic, political, and social developments created the space for an expanded black middle class in the 1970s.[31] As exiles with the temptation of assimilation ever before them, many in this educated, professionally astute segment of the black community trusted more in their material success and social status than in a Christian faith and a congregational connection. The retreat of many churches into a "period of otherworldliness" following the death of Martin Luther King Jr. and the decentralization of political activism pushed many during this time to seek out spiritual community within Islam[32] or New Age religions.

By the mid–1980s and early 1990s, however, after raising a generation of black children who were not intimately connected to a community of faith, many successful middle-class blacks began to return to or enter churches for the first time. They sought meaning and belonging that was elusive at best in the corridors of corporate America or their suburban neighborhoods. Many black congregations provided what Cheryl Townsend Gilkes calls, "therapeutic relief" from the stresses, strains, and contradictions of being black in white America.[33] But she also notes that the "larger education and talent of the black middle class meant a larger pool of talent available to serve their churches."[34] This educated laity, which experienced a semblance of self-determination and autonomy, and which was often inspired by the spirit of the Black Power movement, sought to control their churches and communities, and they built strong black institutions. But despite the measurable growth of the black middle class in the decades following the civil rights movement, there grew a widening gap between the middle class and their sisters and brothers on or below the poverty line. This prompted many congregations to collectively address the issues of education, housing, and economic development through new businesses and jobs.

It was during this post–civil rights/post–Black Power era, consequently, when many sought ways to rediscover the black religious tradition, most pointedly through worship, music, and the display of black art. They essentially rediscovered the black church as a social and cultural center.[35] Within their midst, there were a number of congregations that adjusted their cultural lenses to see pride in their black heritage as well as power in a more explicit African identity. It was, moreover, during the late 1980s and the early 1990s that many new congregations sought a cultural identity while others, which were already "black and proud," moved to another level of consciousness. Through the lenses of their African identity, they saw the need to capitalize on their collective gifts and resources, to address critical issues, and to enhance and empower black communities. This moved them from simply knowing about Africa to being African, starting from a historical locus on the margins to occupying an ontological location at the center.

Before concluding this introduction, it is important to understand how the phrase "walkin' the talk and keepin' the faith" is seen in the life of Africentric congregations. To walk the talk is to live out the cultural values and convictions that one professes. This is good in an African-centered congregational context because it motivates a response to life from a specific cultural self-understanding with its accompanying system of values. The danger of an emphasis on walking the talk of cultural identity alone is that it focuses on only one way of being and runs the risk of mirroring the very Eurocentricity that has kept non-Europeans trapped in categories of inferiority. In essence, to walk the talk of cultural identity alone creates a worldview that separates and marginalizes.

To keep the faith is to be intentionally and constantly convicted by the mandates of one's faith. This is good in an African-centered congregational context because it uses one's faith tradition as a yardstick to measure all reflections, critiques, and actions. The danger of only keeping the faith, however, is that it can create a kind of "religious tunnel-vision" or myopic way of viewing the world that has no place for new kinds of reflection, new levels of critique, or new modes of action. Congregations with a firm grounding in their doctrine and practice, for example, keep the faith in ways that have been passed down for generations. Unfortunately, in some cases, this faith has become insensitive to and unshaken by the changes in culture and thought. But when congregations combine their cultural walk with their faith talk, they bring forth a creative tension that keeps faith and culture in balance. They realize that they should not live out values and convictions that are not measured by the demands of faith; likewise, their faith must always find concrete, reflective expression in transformative action. It is, therefore, the use of this phrase in a congregational context that provides the basic framework for an Africentric spirituality in black congregations that is balanced and accountable.

Because a congregation's collective story is a key part of its culture and the major point of reference for its ministry focus, this book will profile three churches that self-identify as Africentric. Using the tools of interviewing, observation, data collection, casual conversation, and spending focused time at each site as a participant-observer, I gathered a variety of data that revealed three enlightening and empowering congregational stories. Together they uncover yet another level of what it means to be black and Christian in America. In chapter 1, I draw the boundaries of this discussion by defining American spirituality and African American spirituality and describing the emergent contours for an Africentric spirituality within congregations. I also introduce the restated descriptions of the Nguzo Saba, which provide the lenses for examining how each congregation walks the talk and keeps the faith in an African-centered context. Chapter 2 profiles Imani Temple Christian Fellowship of Pomona, California, a small, 380-member congregation founded in 1998. It examines the ways that Imani enfolds the principles of Creativity and Collective Work and Responsibility into its ministry and commitment. Chapter 3 features First Afrikan Presbyterian Church of Lithonia, Georgia, a medium-sized, nine-hundred-member congregation. The embodiment of the principles of Cooperative Economics and Self-Determination are explored as they are found in the ministry and vision of this ten-year-old congregation. Chapter 4 tells the story of Trinity United Church of Christ of Chicago, Illinois, a forty-one-year-old congregation with more than eight thousand members as it lives out the principles of Unity and Purpose in its ministry and mission. Each congregational chapter begins with a historical profile followed by a discussion of the embodiment of the selected principles of the Nguzo Saba as interpretive lenses. Chapter 5 brings the entire discussion under the principle of Faith, while Chapter 6 provides questions and insights that will invite pastors and lay leaders to explore the implications of these values and commitments for their own congregation's life and ministry.

It is important to point out that these congregations intentionally represent diversity in size, age, location, and affiliation in an effort to illustrate multiple expressions of Africentric ministry. They also find membership outside of the seven largest historically black denominations. Trinity UCC and First Afrikan Presbyterian are black congregations within white mainstream denominations, while Imani Temple claims no denominational affiliation. I believe that their ecclesial locations provide important lenses through which to view black religion in congregational contexts that have had limited but growing scholarly attention. This book, therefore, highlights, explores, and discusses representative examples of congregations that have tapped into the richness of their African heritage. It also suggests ways of creating a framework for an African-centered spirituality that is one of several meaningful ways to be Christians of African descent in America. It is my hope that this study will open the way for a deeper and broader understanding of and appreciation for the diversity of the American religious landscape in general and black religious traditions more specifically.

one

Moving Toward an Africentric Spirituality

AMERICAN SPIRITUALITY

In a *New York Times Magazine* article dated December 12, 1997, Jack Miles declared, "Religion Makes a Comeback."[1] The article goes on to state that in America, recent attitudes toward religion are changing and interest in religion is increasing. This can be substantiated by statistics that reveal a surge in the number of people seeking a spiritual connection from 58 percent in 1994 to 82 percent in 1998.[2] It is also evidenced by the growth, at least in conservative circles, of "seeker," "mall," and "cell" churches[3] that provide clear, unambiguous teaching that limits choice and attempts to provide a sense of rootedness in a rapidly changing society. It is important to note that this interest in religion does not simply mean people are joining or returning to churches but that many are searching for a greater sense of God in their lives, outside of a traditional religious institution. This yearning, says sociologist Robert Wuthnow, is related to the need to make sense of life in an increasingly secular society as one holds on to an undeniable belief in the existence of God.[4] This points to more than religious revival but to a yearning for spiritual fulfillment. The real question, however, that lays the foundation for this discussion is: What is spirituality?

Contemporary scholars of this subject will concur that spirituality is a difficult concept to define. The word itself in many languages refers to the elusiveness and mystery of wind and breath as seen in the Greek and Latin. It is something that clearly exists but cannot be contained. It is something that can provide unity but cannot be fully captured. Steve Jacobsen in his book *Heart to God, Hands to Work: Connecting Spirituality and Work* says that "spirituality is a relationship to something beyond myself that is intangible but also real."[5] He goes on to say that it is the source of one's value and meaning in life, one's understanding of the world, an awareness of one's inner self, and a need to create and sustain an integrated self. It could be concluded, then, that regardless of one's commitment to a religious institution, all human beings, by their very nature, possess spiritual longings that require fulfillment in some form or another.

In light of the more general understanding of spirituality, Wuthnow suggests that there has been a "profound change" in the spiritual practices of Americans. He argues that this change is seen in the movement from a "spirituality of dwelling" to a "spirituality of seeking."[6] He defines the former as one that requires, "sharp symbolic boundaries to protect sacred space from its surroundings." He further characterizes it as the more traditional form of "habitation" or an experience of trust that one has in a specific notion of sacred space that the Divine creates and in which the Divine resides. This resembles a more static understanding of life and the spirit. The spirituality of seeking, on the other hand, requires one to seek and find sacred moments that reinforce one's convictions that the Divine exists.[7] This need for reinforcement is in light of the swift transition within American society and it leads to a person's freedom to create or negotiate the kind of God/human connection space that suits an individual's lifestyle. In earlier decades of the twentieth century, for example, people gathered in churches with like-minded worshippers for a familiar and often traditional experience of honoring God, and it was in this setting that they could dwell with the Holy. As the years progressed, however, and the issues and challenges in society have changed, many congregations have attempted to adapt to these shifts in an effort to keep up with the times. The result has been a new freedom that gives license for individuals to look for and find the particular innovation that best supports their lifestyle and beliefs.

While each of these may accurately describe the reality of American spirituality, Wuthnow suggests a third alternative that he believes is more appropriate for twenty-first-century life, which he calls, "practice-oriented spirituality."[8] It differs from a spirituality of dwelling that may take the existence of God for granted or a spirituality of seeking that allows any combination of experience to constitute a God-focused relationship. It requires the cultivation of intentional spiritual practices like prayer and meditation that are not simply a means to an end but that provide the foundation for a way of life. He believes that this third alternative to contemporary American spirituality is the next logical step from a seeking-oriented spirituality because it provides a "more orderly, disciplined and focused approach to the sacred."[9] It is also an improvement on a spirituality of dwelling because it gives a more "balanced perspective of the sacredness of the world" that does not restrict or confine the meaning of sacred space.[10] This kind of spirituality also cultivates a commitment to service toward others in response to a deepening relationship with God.[11]

American spirituality at this point in history is clearly diverse in its expressions and experiences and the trends indicate a move toward both individual and corporate innovation. A spirituality of practice, for Wuthnow, is a way to reinforce and sustain one's spiritual life and to enrich the lives of others through service. Within the midst of this evolution of spirituality in America, and in light of our discussion centering on African American congregations and spirituality, the question remains: Is there a distinctive spiritual expression among African American congregations?

AFRICAN AMERICAN SPIRITUALITY

The answer to this question is a resounding "yes" as seen in the insights on the subject found in *Hidden Wholeness: An African American Spirituality for Individuals and Communities,* by Michael I. N. Dash, Jonathan Jackson, and Stephen C. Rasor. They argue that spirituality from an African American perspective is special "because it grows out of the experience of a unique people of color who have encountered a God who sustains and liberates."[12] They go on to say that it provides the basis for wholeness. It is important to note that this spiritual resource does not begin with the slave experience in America but goes back to the worldview and sensibilities of African spiritualities. They are clear to point out that African American spirituality is not a carbon copy of its continental counterparts, for an important transformation took place through the process and experiences of capture and enslavement that created a new and distinctive form.

In line with Melville Herskovitz and others who contend that a significant amount of "Africanisms" were retained by African captives, they identify certain "trace elements" of that spirituality that provide a continuity between experiences in Africa, slavery, and on to the present.[13] They include a sense of a unified cosmos, and an understanding of God as "creator of the universe and human beings, transcendent of divine power, preserver of all life, and the final authority and arbiter in all matters."[14] There is also a profound significance placed on communalism. This is lived out in the realization that the community and its members and not the individual is the starting place for awareness and empowerment of the self.[15] In the book *Black Spirituality and Black Consciousness: Soul Force, Culture, and Freedom in the African-American Experience,* Carlyle F. Stewart III affirms this connection between community and spirituality found in the daily lives of African Americans. He emphasizes the value of human freedom that results from cooperative and harmonious relationships on the basis of black *communitas.*[16] Together, these elements of divine presence and human communality have provided the platform on which African Americans have not only survived but thrived. Through a shared history of suffering, oppression, and liberation, African Americans have cultivated a collective strength and vitality that is only possible through the power of a liberating God.

In his book *Another Day's Journey: Black Churches Confronting the American Crisis,* Robert M. Franklin places spirituality into a congregational context with a helpful topology of the traditions of African American spirituality.[17] He describes seven spiritual traditions and their accompanying practices as "major styles of thought" about spirituality in African American congregations. He begins with an Evangelical style that focuses on the knowledge of God's Word through the disciplines of teaching, preaching, and studying. Next he identifies the Holiness tradition, whose purpose is purity of life and thought through the practices of fasting, praying, and renunciation, as well as a Charismatic tradition that is experienced through the spirit as it encourages tarrying and seeking spiritual gifts. He then moves on to the Social Justice and Afrocentric traditions; the former emphasizes public righteousness through activism and the latter celebrates African heritage through the display of culture. He completes his topology with the Contemplative tradition, whose end is to seek intimacy with God through the experiences of prayer and meditation, and, finally, with New Age tradition that pursues peace of mind through the practices of meditation, chanting, and music.

These seven spiritual traditions of the black church give us a closer look at common spiritual practices of the black religious tradition.[18] The disciplines of fasting, tarrying, chanting, and meditation center on individual growth and development and complement Wuthnow's spirituality of practice with its emphasis on individual intentionality. On the other hand, teaching, preaching, activism, cultural display, and the nurture of gifts that are more outward and communal expressions of the inward spirit echo the more specific spirituality discussed by Dash, Jackson, and Rasor. I would go so far as to say that together these spiritual traditions, as described by Franklin, have been uniquely effective toward the survival of the black church as it supports important and sustaining spiritual practices.

So if these definitions and explanations describe African American spirituality, what is Africentric spirituality? How is it experienced in African American congregations? How is it different from other forms of spirituality? To answer these questions, I look to the Nguzo Saba or Seven Principles of Kwanzaa as interpretive lenses. For more than thirty years, African American congregations across the nation have practiced Kwanzaa in a variety of forms. In each case, they have recognized the importance of upholding specific principles as markers to guide their congregational life and ministry. Through the familiar principles of Unity, Self-Determination, Collective Work and Responsibility, Cooperative Economics, Purpose, Creativity, and Faith,[19] I believe we see a glimpse of the contours of an Africentric spirituality that moves congregations from simply celebrating their African heritage to being Africans in the context of American religious life.

This spirituality is accessible to all African American congregations by virtue of their heritage and location. In light of a collective history that moves from autonomy in Africa to captivity and oppression in America, they each have the opportunity to live out their ministries in the spirit of Sankofa as they look back to recall and recount the past in an effort to be empowered to move forward. Most African American congregations today acknowledge and celebrate their past as they look to the future. African-centered congregations do this as well but, when they look back, they do so with a mind for cultural heritage as well as spiritual empowerment.

Rather than simply recounting and celebrating the accomplishments of the great women and men in African and African American history, they actually claim the power and presence of the ancestors. Rather than merely acknowledging a historical and spiritual connection with Africa and its people, they name themselves as Africans in Diaspora. Essentially, Africentric congregations seriously and intentionally seek ways to reconcile the tension between their faith and culture—their Africanness and their Christianity. They do this with a mind of those who are in exile; therefore, surviving and thriving requires them to connect both historically and ontologically to Africa and its peoples and culture while living in America. This places Africa at the center of their self-understanding and it shapes all that they do including their religious experience and expression. These congregations reappropriate aspects of the African worldview and sensibilities, recognizing the value of its spirituality in their quest to survive as well as thrive in American society.

WALKIN' THE TALK OF THE NGUZO SABA

I was introduced to the Nguzo Saba or Seven Principles in the mid-1970s when the annual celebration of Kwanzaa began in my local congregation. Over the years, I have looked to them as core values to support Christian education programs, curriculum, and activities as examples of how to walk the talk and keep the faith. But when I began to consider how these principles more explicitly connect faith and culture, I was compelled to research their origins.

I discovered that the development of Kwanzaa by Maulana Karenga in 1966 came out of the Kawaida ideology, which is "a theory of culture and social change that draws from and synthesizes the best in Nationalist, Pan Africanist and socialist thought."[20] The basic concept of Kawaida centered on the contention that "the key crisis in Black life is the cultural crisis" of both views and values. The solution for Karenga and other like-minded scholars was to affirm an "authentic African spirituality rooted in and reflective of an equally authentic African sacred text."[21] This text, *The Husia,* an ancient Kemetic (Egyptian) book of sacred wisdom, was viewed as the foundation upon which to build a spiritual and moral life for Africans in Diaspora. It was, consequently, out of the ideology of Kawaida and the wisdom of *The Husia* that the Seven Principles of Kwanzaa were developed. Their purpose was to advocate a "communitarian African value system necessary to build community and serve as social glue and moral orientation for cultural practice."[22] Kwanzaa was thus established as a holiday that ritually celebrates the African family, community, and culture and serves as a fundamental way of reinforcing the bond between African peoples.[23]

This was indeed a most appropriate response to the social and political context of the 1960s and 1970s and is still so necessary for a people who have been systematically and continually oppressed and denied both their humanity and their rights. Over the past thirty to thirty-five years, however, some congregations have rejected Kwanzaa because of the apparent connection to black nationalism and a perceived notion that it only encourages an ideology of separation and exclusivity among African Americans. But others have embraced it as a way to ritualize their emerging understandings of black theology through a celebration of values that have the potential to bring unity among African Americans. For the purpose of this book, the Nguzo Saba of Kwanzaa will be reconsidered outside of their annual ritualistic format. They will be envisioned as values that enhance and support the goal of keeping the faith by bringing together faith and culture as a potential foundation for an Africentric spirituality.

The first step in their use is to relocate the principle of Faith from being simply one of the seven cultural values to being the foundation for the other six. Karenga says faith is: "To believe with all our heart in our people, our parents, our teachers, our leaders, and the righteousness and victory of our struggle."[24] This is, indeed, a strong statement that affirms the important part Faith plays in the strengthening of social, political, and cultural identity. Within the context of African American Christian congregations, however, it is imperative that Faith as a foundational principle is explicitly connected to a liberating theology whose hope is in the transforming power of Christ. I will, consequently, use Faith as the linchpin to connect the other six principles. Recognizing that each principle must be grounded in faith and find its expression in the cultural realities of black congregational life, I will also restate the working definitions of the Seven Principles to reflect both the cultural and theological realities of African American Christians. In this way, these principles serve as a bridge to unite a faith rooted in the liberating gospel of Jesus Christ and a culture centered in the crucible of African and African American reality/experience. I offer, then, a reappropriation of the Nguzo Saba that I believe opens the way to a fuller and more appropriate system of values for African-centered congregations for the twenty-first century, by acknowledging the cultural reality as well as the religious/theological commitment.

Unity

Karenga states that this first principle is *"to strive for and maintain unity in the family, community and race."*[25] He begins intentionally with the family as the most intimate social unit and then moves on to embrace the community and the race. Unity as both principle and practice, he states, is "harmonious togetherness, not simply a being together." He further describes it as "active solidarity" rooted in positive interaction that ultimately brings people together as a family, community, or nation through a connectedness grounded in a consciously shared identity.[26] This understanding of Unity is essentially relational and it connects across familial, generational, and community lines. It is clearly a strong example of "walkin' the talk" for any Africentric congregation because it is solidly based in the communitarian framework of the African worldview and it opens the way for moral and ethical actions based on mutuality and harmony.

In the context of the congregational life, however, this effort to walk the talk is fortified when viewed through the eyes of Faith. Any effort toward Unity of family, community, or race in a congregational context denies its full potential if it does not find the true origin of its uniting power in its relationship to the God of creation and the Christ of redemption. With this in mind, I redefine Unity as the effort *to seek and maintain unity that begins with our relationship with God, affirms our connection to Africa and the Diaspora, and calls forth solidarity among and liberation for all of God's people.* Through this renewed description, we are reminded that it was God who spoke a word and brought a uniting order out of chaos in Genesis 1:1–22. And it was Christ whose act of incarnation united humanity with divinity, bringing the possibility of life and liberty to all God's people as witnessed in the Gospels. Through both vertical and horizontal relationships, Unity becomes fuller and more holistic as a congregation allows its identity in God to inform interactions with its members and those in the community. But it is important to note that this kind of genuine Unity involves the risk of stepping outside of self-centered perceptions and attitudes and becoming open to new ways of thinking and being. A congregation that walks the talk of Unity, therefore, must ground its togetherness in a love that unites and supports active solidarity across lines of gender, class, race, sexual orientation, and faith traditions, for the mutual benefit and liberation of all. In the spirit of Galatians 3:28, this Unity affirms that there is "no longer Jew or Greek, . . . slave or free, . . . male and female; for all of you are one in Christ Jesus."

Self-Determination

When Karenga describes the second principle, he affirms that it means *"to define ourselves, name ourselves, create for ourselves and speak for ourselves."*[27] Here he focuses on the important process of defining one's identity. Building on the teachings of Frantz Fanon, he believes that Self-Determination should answer three questions: "Who am I?" "Am I really who I am?" and "Am I all I ought to be?" Answering the first in the spirit of Self-Determination links one to a knowledge of history and culture, the second to a collective identity that authenticates what is real and unreal, and the third to standards of ethical and cultural excellence that govern practice and thought.[28] This emphasis on a self-determined identity provides a solid grounding for Africentric congregations. It not only celebrates individual and communal achievements, it also gives the freedom to define, create, and respond to the needs and challenges of African peoples as well as the hopes and visions in their distinctive realities.

In the context of congregational life, however, walking the talk of Self-Determination becomes a powerful motivation for action when it is seen through the lens of Faith. Because of the foibles of human nature, any effort toward self-affirmation becomes narrow and narcissistic if it does not emanate from a higher source. Defining, naming, creating, and speaking both individually and corporately get stuck in myopic agendas that create a spirit of exclusivism and internal division. In response to this, a renewed definition of Self-Determination is *to define ourselves as daughters and sons of Africa, created in the image of God, and willing to participate in the liberation of those in the Diaspora and the world.* In this light, an additional question to be added to Karenga's inquiry about identity is "Whose am I?" The appropriate answer, in light of the renewed definition, has the power to shift a narrow, utilitarian Self-Determination into one that finds its defining moment as a child of God, affirming that it is "[God] who has made us and not we ourselves" (Ps. 100:3a NAS). From this point of reference, tendencies toward self-hatred are neutralized in the knowledge that everything God created is good, as stated in Genesis, and that the message of God's love is for "whosoever." Congregations that walk the talk of Self-Determination must, therefore, recover lost memory and boldly shape a world around communal images and interests. But this all must be grounded in the knowledge of and modeled after Christ, who, in the ultimate act of Self-Determination, gave himself for us all.

Collective Work and Responsibility

For Karenga, this principle is *"to build and maintain our community together and make our brother's and sister's problems our problems and to solve them together."*[29] This third principle states that no progress toward liberation is possible unless a people work and struggle together for the good of all. Within this understanding of Collective Work and Responsibility, he says that "African is not just an identity but also a destiny and duty." It is important to note that this destiny is built on both collective failures and victories and implies an openness to "self-criticism" and "self-correction" for the betterment of all.[30] This principle, as with the others, draws from an African communal worldview that encourages the sharing of both joy

10

and pain and is an indispensable concept for any Africentric congregation as it walks the talk of Collective Work and Responsibility.

When seen through the eyes of Faith, however, this principle speaks to the realities of congregational life in the twenty-first century through an example of service and mutual accountability seen in the first-century church. The challenge of this principle came forth quite vividly in the disagreement surrounding the care of the widows in Acts 6. Once the disparity between service and evangelism was identified, a mutual solution was created to share labor for the good of all. This concrete example of Collective Work and Responsibility is revealed in the way they resolved the problem through the spirit of cooperation and consideration. Moving from the first to the twenty-first century and to the hopes and challenges of contemporary congregations, we see a new definition of this principle. It is *to build and maintain our communities as Africans in Diaspora who live in a context of service and mutual accountability in America and the world, strengthened by the liberating spirit of God.* It reminds us that the church is the body of Christ, where each separate part, wherever it is found in the world, has honor in its own right yet is incomplete outside of the work of the whole. Just as the hand is no greater than the foot, those in the choir stand have no greater presence than those in the kitchen. A congregation that walks the talk of Collective Work and Responsibility, therefore, must affirm the indivisibility of the communal self while embracing the presence of God's spirit that strengthens all in the struggle and brings wholeness to the entire body of Christ.

Cooperative Economics

For Karenga the fourth principle means *"to build and maintain our own stores, shops and other businesses and to profit from them together."* It centers on a "commitment to the practice of shared social wealth and the work necessary to achieve it."[31] Much like Collective Work and Responsibility, this principle stresses the importance of responsibility and accountability within the community. Cooperative Economics, however, presents a more explicit value that cautions the misuse of social wealth that results in an inequality exploitive of the poor and marginalized. This principle, therefore, upholds an "ethic of care and responsibility [that is] expressed in the concept of shared wealth and service to the most disadvantaged."[32] For Africentric congregations, it is essential that they harness the collective resources and use them *in* the community through a passionate concern about the equitable use of wealth *for* the community.

In the contemporary congregational context, however, the concept of wealth seen through the eyes of Faith must be broadened to include all manner of resources. It is too easy for a congregation to believe that they have fully embodied this principle when they build or sponsor "shops, stores and businesses" that keep the money in their community. A new definition of Cooperative Economics is *to believe in and demonstrate a holistic, multidimensional stewardship that values all our resources, including material, human, intellectual, and spiritual, as gifts to us from God to be developed and used in African American communities, the Diaspora, and the world for the good of all people.* In light of this renewed description, the greater challenge is to view Cooperative Economics as the efficient and effective use of our God-given resources in the work and leadership of a congregation in its community as well as the world. This use does not exploit others based on their lack of education or income but provides ways to affirm and celebrate the diversity of their gifts.

A concrete example is seen in the composition of those who followed Jesus as disciples. These women and men came from a variety of occupations and vocations—from Martha as the consummate homemaker to Peter as a common fisherman and on to Luke as a skilled physician. Each brought valuable gifts that contributed equally to the teaching and dissemination of the gospel. In the use of these gifts, however, the disciples also learned the importance of honoring and respecting all gifts as the collective resources of the community. Moreover, a congregation that walks the talk of Cooperative Economics must understand the value of collective resources and provide opportunities for their use and further development for the collective good.

Purpose

Karenga states that this fifth principle is *"to make our collective vocation the building and developing of our community in order to restore our people to their traditional greatness."* He purports that it is a "commitment to the collective vocation" of African people through their shared legacy. This legacy is not simply for knowledge's sake but as an "overriding cultural purpose [that] suggests a direction," and points to a common destiny. Borrowing from Mary McLeod Bethune, he states three facts about such a Purpose.

The first and second are that it designates African people as both heirs and custodians of a great legacy. As heirs they receive and value the legacy but as custodians their duty is to "guard, preserve, expand and promote it."[33] The third acknowledges the destiny of African peoples as major players in human history[34] and anticipates a continuing destiny of greatness and accomplishment in that history. These are indeed welcome words of affirmation for Africentric congregations, for it deepens their sense of communal vocation and commitment by tying it to a great and honorable past that expects a great and honorable future.

In the context of congregational life and ministry, however, this sense of Purpose and destiny remains narrow and disconnected from the larger world community if one does not also add the mandate of the gospel when seen through the eyes of Faith. A renewed definition is *to build and develop our communities in ways that acknowledge the sacredness of our collective work of liberation in the Diaspora, and the world and our dependence on God's power and grace to perform it.* Hence, Purpose as a collective vocation must be directed by the divine destiny of a God of inclusion and love. Jesus, for example, did not restrict the spread of the gospel to Jerusalem in Acts 1:7–8 but commanded that it also flow to Judea, to Samaria, and even to the ends of the earth. It is important to note that, well aware of the geographic and cultural challenges that this kind of evangelism would spawn, before the command he promised the disciples that they would "receive power when the Holy Spirit has come upon you" (Acts 1:8a). It was through this divine assistance that they were able to attempt such an ambitious task and fulfill their intended destiny. Likewise, living the African legacy as heirs and custodians in a world that has historically and continually defamed this legacy will require Faith in and dependence on a God of liberation and justice. Congregations that walk the talk of Purpose, moreover, must be committed to give witness to the hard truths that support a commitment to justice and liberation for all.

Creativity

The sixth principle follows logically from Purpose, says Karenga, as it places emphasis on "restoring African people to traditional greatness and revitalizing the community for greater work and service." He says it is *"to do always as much as we can, in the way that we can in order to leave our community more beautiful and beneficial than we inherited it."*[35] In this view, Creativity is both an original act and a restorative act in imitation of the Creator. The goals of this creative thrust are "affirming truth, justice, harmony, righteousness, balance, order and rightness" which are embodied in the Egyptian concept of MAAT.[36] This "creative restoration" is seen as valuable in both the context of ancient Egypt as well as contemporary African American life, and the purpose, says Karenga, is to leave a "legacy which builds on and enriches the legacy before us."[37] This principle, therefore, centers on the notion of communal wholeness that extends across generations and millennia. For Africentric congregations, this notion of Creativity moves them to acknowledge and celebrate their African legacy as well as devise ways to reappropriate it imaginatively for contemporary living.

In the context of congregational life, however, Creativity must begin with a "restorative revitalization" of individual and corporate relationships with God when viewed through the lenses of Faith. Moving beyond routine and superficial prayer and praise, congregations must use every impulse of their being for fuller worship and greater service. The renewed definition that affirms that movement is *to ground our creative energy in a renewed and renewing relationship with God that restores African American communities and creates new possibilities for commitment to the Diaspora and the world for the benefit of all people.* Here we link a kind of "restorative revitalization" that is at the core of the resurrection, for the legacy of Jesus of Nazareth finds its greatest and most liberating energy in Jesus the Christ, the risen Savior. This resurrection power is not reserved for the life to come but is also manifested in the creativity of the Spirit that comforts as well as empowers today. For congregations that walk the talk of Creativity this is not simply believing in the resurrected Christ but living a life of revitalized potential that receives the personal promise of eternal life in the hereafter and also engages in the communal struggle for justice and liberation in this life.

Faith

In his description of the final principle, Karenga views it as the appropriate closing for a series of principles that began with Unity. He says it is *"to believe with all our heart in our people, our parents, our teachers, our leaders, and the righteousness and victory of our struggle."* "Without Unity," he says, "we cannot begin our most important work, but without Faith we cannot sustain it." Although the description itself makes no mention of God, Karenga implies the divine presence of the Creator God that is a part of African spiritualities. He uses this starting point as the catalyst that propels humankind into the forefront of the discussion, created in the image of God, and therefore "capable of ultimate righteousness and creativity through self-mastery and development in the context of positive support."[38] This understanding of human potential leads to a kind of humanism that values faith in one's self as key. This emphasis on believing in the potential of the black community undergirds the previous principles that bolster self-esteem and support self-confidence in the life of Africentric congregations as they struggle to walk the talk of Faith.

In the context of a liberating gospel that is grounded in God's love and power, however, congregations must understand the difference between having faith and keeping the faith. Having faith is declaring strong belief, but keeping the faith puts that belief into concrete action. A renewed definition that supports the latter is, then, *to always look to and depend upon the presence and power of the reconciling and liberating spirit of God that transforms what we say, do, think, and dream beyond our imagination for the benefit of all creation.*

Jesus' threefold question to Peter in John 21:15 tests this kind of faith when he asks, "Do you love me?" Although Peter replied with a hearty "yes I do!" the true test of his faith would come in Peter's willingness to follow the command, "Feed my lambs" and to also die the death of Christ. In a similar manner, congregations that profess a Faith in their capacity for "ultimate righteousness and creativity through self-mastery," alone give only lip service to Jesus' question, "Do you love me?" But a Faith that finds its locus in God and uses the creativity of a diverse and rich African heritage has the foundation needed to truly "feed" God's lambs.

Congregations that walk the talk of Faith, informed by the sense of communality, affirmation, and destiny found in Unity, Self-Determination, Collective Work and Responsibility, Cooperative Economics, Purpose, and Creativity, place the possibilities of human potential into the hands of God for greater works of ministry and service. These restated principles, as they are drawn from a spirituality centered on the African notions of harmony and divine presence, create the contours of an African-centered spirituality that walks the talk of Faith.

15

KEEPIN' THE FAITH IN A CONGREGATIONAL CONTEXT

In 1992, the Kelly Miller Smith Institute of Vanderbilt University sought answers to the challenges of keeping the faith through the "doing" of theology as it launched a national dialogue entitled "What Does It Mean to Be Black and Christian?" Following the initial consultation between professional theologians and church leaders, there was a series of forums and seminars held across the country for the next five years, whereby local church leaders were invited to join in the conversation.

An important point of departure for this consultation was the publication of volumes 1 and 2 of *What Does It Mean to Be Black and Christian? Pulpit, Pew and Academy in Dialogue.*[39] They presented collections of essays that addressed these major issues and were designed to facilitate a much-needed dialogue within congregations in an effort to encourage and support ministries of liberation and transformation. I attended the forum held in my area in 1996 and was inspired to use the title question as a point of discussion in one of the chapters in my doctoral dissertation. I agreed, as stated in the preface of volume 1, that the title question was a response to an identity crisis that begins to find answers as the academy and church build bridges connecting each other. In more recent years, however, I have come to believe that a model that begins with a reflection on theological discourse, in the hope that it will encourage more purposeful action, is insufficient when used alone. Simultaneous attention must also be given to the work in local congregations that provide concrete actions that illustrate and appropriate the context of theology. This presupposes an active presence of theology in the pews, hence my emphasis on the life and ministry of congregations. But the marriage between local congregations and black theology is not as easy as it seems.

In the essay "Black Theology in Praxis" (included in *Black and Christian* volume 1), Dennis Wiley explores the questions surrounding the implementation of black theology in African American congregations.[40] He describes briefly the movement of black theology from an initial attack on the white church and its theology to a sharp critique of the black church and on to its move into the realm of an academic discipline. Although black theology contains implications for practice, he points out the lack of "how-to" and "step-by-step" guides to help congregations "transform Black theological theory into Black congregational *praxis*."[41] I concur that this movement from thinking to doing, from theory to practice, from the academy to the local church is indeed important. I believe, however, that there is equal value in beginning with the practices of local congregations and then moving on to an active theological reflection.

In the book *Practicing Our Faith: A Way of Life for a Searching People,* Dorothy Bass describes practices as, "A way of thinking about life, [that] addresses fundamental human needs and conditions through concrete humans acts."[42] She goes on to describe them as being practical, interrelated, done together over time, and possessing standards of excellence; but, more importantly for the congregational context, they are infused with the divine. It follows then that the task before us is not to "transform Black theological theory into Black congregational praxis," but to identify and examine the sustaining practices of African-centered congregations through lenses of both theology and practice—faith and culture. Africentric spirituality then emerges within these congregations when they actively and intentionally rename and claim the transformed sensibilities of African spirituality and engage in practices that reflect their faith/culture response as they "do" black theology.

Embedded in the stories of the three congregations I profile in the next three chapters, we find representative examples of how their practice of spirituality is lived out in their mission and ministry. These stories also reveal diversity in their African-centeredness influenced by their varying size, age, geography, theology, and affiliation. Hence, they give witness to the fact that there are many ways to be Africentric, reflecting the creative genius of their God, but they all share the value of communality and a Pan-African spirit. I contend further that the Nguzo Saba, when seen as expanded principles that partner both culture and faith, provides a glimpse of an Africentric spirituality that is present in these congregations. This spirituality, in turn, becomes the foundation for holistic and empowering witness and service in these congregations that tries to maintain a creative balance between culture and faith.

The three identified congregations intentionally self-identify as African-centered as they share two foundational values of an African-centered identity. The first value is a Diaspora consciousness that embraces a broadened sense of community, and the second is a commitment to maintain harmony between the sacred and secular, faith and culture. Although the congregations share common values and sensibilities, their expressions and experiences grow out of their distinctive interpretation of what it means to be black and Christian. Imani Temple, for example, draws strength from an evangelistic mandate of outreach; First Afrikan finds value in an interpretation of black Christian nationalism; and Trinity is motivated by the spirit of social activism. It is, moreover, within the stories of each of these congregations that we find a glimpse of the creative genius of a God who invites them to consider both the gift and challenge of being Christians of African descent in America. As a people in exile, Africentric congregations are learning that their Christian practices alone are not enough. They need a worldview that supports their humanity, nurtures their spirituality, and promises their liberation. They each are accepting the challenge of walking the talk and keeping the faith as the sun-kissed daughters and sons of Africa who find themselves in America.

two

Imani Temple Christian Fellowship

Collective Work and Responsibility and Creativity

THE CONGREGATIONAL STORY

There were twenty people in attendance on July 19, 1998, the first worship service of the Imani Temple Christian Fellowship in Pomona, California. This small but spirited group did not assemble in a traditional church building but in a home.[1] They did not sit on padded pews but on metal folding chairs. There was no background music from a piano or organ, only selected songs from a CD. There were no hymnals or music sheets, only praise songs taught by the pastor. But despite the absence of the traditional elements of worship, there was a spirit of anticipation in the air that warm July morning. Those who gathered that day came from many different backgrounds and experiences but they all sought a place where they could find spiritual wholeness and receive a genuine encounter with God. Little did they know that this search would result in an expanded notion of community through experiences and expressions of Collective Work/Responsibility and Creativity. One clear example of this quest and its results is seen through the eyes of a woman in her mid-thirties who joined Imani in 1999.

Although she was not raised in the church as a young adult, Monette Rayford, a.k.a. Mo, moved between Baptist, Church of Christ, and Jehovah's Witness congregations searching for spiritual fulfillment, or what she called a "high."[2] "My previous church experience didn't hold me because I got tired of watchin' phony Christians talk about Christ but didn't allow him to move in their lives," she recalled. She witnessed many people, "getting their shout on," but this was often in direct conflict with hypocritical attitudes and behaviors outside of the sanctuary. "There was a lot of religion going on but no authentic praise," she added. In these congregations she felt judged more by the length of her skirt and the absence of a professional title than by the sincerity in her heart and her thirst for God. Then in June 1999, she was invited by a friend to attend Imani Temple. When she heard that they met in a house, she laughed and said, "I ain't going to no church that's in a house." But after hearing the excitement of her friend she changed her mind. "I just had to go, see, hear, and witness this spirit that she had been telling me about." So she gave it a try. After all, she was looking for something different and this was clearly outside of her realm of experience. Once she got beyond the physical location, Mo began to experience a sense of freedom like never before.

The focus on outward appearance and presentation she experienced in other churches took a back seat in Imani's humble surroundings. She discovered a spirit deep within that emerged and connected her with other worshipers in an experience of community she had never had before. Although not a product of a consistent religious community, she was familiar with the movement of the Spirit in her life. Over the previous nineteen years, Mo had written a variety of poems inspired by a deep stirring within, and at Imani she was elated to discover that this form of expression was welcomed. Imani unlocked a door to her spirit that gave her license to create and recreate using words and images that found their source in God. But Mo also learned that creativity goes beyond artistic expression and includes the restoration of wholeness that renews minds and changes lives. This emerging sense of wholeness made an important difference in the way she understood herself but found its true completion in the collective spirit that was beginning to grow in Imani during these early days.

It was soon after she joined Imani that this small but dedicated group began to search for a new worship site. A vacant warehouse was located in Pomona, but the acquisition of that property did not happen so easily. While the owner was eager to lease the property, he was not so eager to lease it to a church. This reluctance became a major prayer concern for the Imani family so they initiated a three-week prayer vigil that included physically "praying around the walls" of the building and anointing its doors with oil. This spontaneous ritual experience tightened the bond between this band of believers and began to solidify them around a common goal and a collective vision. When the owner finally agreed to sell the building, they shared a new sense of group ownership. It transcended the mere possession of property and contributed to the growing sense of meaning and belonging within the congregation through this early experience of Collective Work/Responsibility.

Once the building was secured, creative renovation converted it into a large sanctuary that seats about 150, two smaller multipurpose meeting rooms, a study for the pastor, and an open reception area that provides additional meeting space. Moving into a new facility was one thing—maintaining it was clearly another. Families were asked to volunteer on a rotating basis to clean the building each week, providing supplies and equipment as well as plenty of elbow grease. Admittedly Mo's initial response to that request was one of complaint, but she and others soon experienced the spirit of Collective Work/Responsibility. Reflecting on that experience, Mo said, "Cleaning the church on Saturday made me feel like, Okay, this is my church, not just the pastor's church. I learned quickly, if not me, then who? I felt like I belonged." She and others discovered that the notion of community emerging at Imani was not based solely on a common physical, socioeconomic, or theological location but more on relationship, collaboration, and accountability. Consequently, the depth of commitment that they experienced in the simple task of maintaining the building created a relational bond that was the embodiment of Collective Work/Responsibility. It was also an illustration of a Creativity that restored and revitalized not only the building but relationships and lives as well. It is this coming together of a commitment to community with a reverence for restoration that became the foundation for Imani Temple, and it compelled many like Mo to join its ranks.

The initial vision for this new church was conceived in the heart of its founding pastor, Jelani Faraja Kafela.[3] It was born with the help of his mother, Muriel Cloyd, and wife, Kathy, as able midwives, and found a nurturing nest among a core of family and friends. "Prior to the initial gathering in 1998," Kafela told me, "I dedicated twenty-five years of service to the cause of juvenile justice in the city of Des Moines and throughout the state of Iowa where I made my home after attending college." He was inspired by study in the Institute for the Advanced Study of Black Family Life and Culture. This institute was founded by noted black psychologist Dr. Wade Nobles, who believed that African philosophy serves as a strong foundation for black psychology and possesses positive features that can bring psychological health and wholeness to Africans in Diaspora.[4] Influenced by Nobles, Kafela later became the founding director of the Baraza Education and Cultural Center, where he established programs that supported spiritual, relational, cultural, and economic advancement of the African American community. "At the Center," he recalled, "we focused especially on the problems of substance abuse, gang violence, and academic failure that plagued the community and threatened the continuity and integrity of people of African descent in America." They also emphasized the importance of cultural values and the cultivation of a communal consciousness that would strengthen African American communities in the spirit of Collective Work/Responsibility and Creativity.

During his travels across the country as a motivational speaker on these issues, Kafela discerned a call to ministry that led him to the position of associate pastor of the Shiloh Missionary Baptist Church in Des Moines, Iowa. "After three years of service," he said, "I became convinced that the church should be a place to plan, develop, and implement programs and networks that would address these concerns. I also became convicted that, for African Americans, this kind of work requires an innovative ministry that combines faith and culture in ways that heal, restore, and empower." Sharing this dream with his wife and mother, he was encouraged to return to Pomona where he grew up and to explore the possibility of planting a new church there. Despite both his fear and reluctance, Mrs. Cloyd recalled with joy that "he led a two-day revival in May of 1998 that attracted many in the community but established a committed core of eight supporters. After the revival, he went back to Des Moines but we anxiously awaited his final return to Pomona." This faithful group met weekly for Bible study of the book of Acts, using materials prepared and sent to them by Kafela. "At our weekly meetings," she continued, "we began to collect our tithes to help establish a financial base for the new ministry." It was this small but motivated group that gathered in the home of the pastor's mother each week that soon became Imani Temple Christian Fellowship.

The dedication and commitment of this "house church" at the end of the twentieth century resembled, in many ways, the early gathering of believers in the weeks and months after Pentecost at the beginning of the first century. They each experienced a sense of connection and mutual accountability that linked individuals through a kinship that transcended biology. Their experiences and expressions of community grew as they met regularly for worship, but ultimately it was their more intimate interactions like feeding the hungry and taking care of the sick that strengthened their bond. The Greek word used by Paul to describe the spirit of such a gathering was *koinonia*.[5] As an adjective it meant common or shared, as a verb it referred to having fellowship, and as a noun it described partners. Together these three uses of the word aptly describe the experience at Imani as a *shared fellowship of partners*. What is distinctive is the way these three characteristics are linked interdependently, supporting and enhancing each other through Collective Work/Responsibility.

During the first month of Imani's life, for example, an elderly, wheelchair-bound man about ninety years old visited several times with his daughter. "One Sunday," recalled Kafela, "this man, whom we began to call Grandpa, told his daughter, 'Roll me up there. I'm join' this preacher!'" This addition to the congregation was seen as a sign of God's grace, because with his presence, Grandpa brought years of wisdom and wholehearted encouragement for the ministry. Because of his age he brought a backward glance that understood the struggles and challenges of being black in America, and through his affirmation he gave validation to the vision that was unfolding into the future. The presence and support from this elder during the early weeks of Imani's life as a congregation became a confirmation of God's blessing and an assurance of God's support.

It was not too long after he joined, however, that Grandpa's health began to decline, restricting him to bed. "For nine months," said Kafela, "the pastoral staff and I visited him regularly for prayer and fellowship, but then he passed away." The brief time shared with Grandpa in worship and at his bedside became an important element in the bond that united this emerging community of faith. As they shared the collective commitment of visitation and the responsible efforts toward fellowship with Grandpa and his family during his final days, their experiences of joy and loss began to lay the foundation for the community of faith they were becoming. This was the beginning of a sense of community for this congregation that extended beyond the grave, required faithfulness and consistency, depended on a collective spirit, and truly sought to live out its name "Imani," which means Faith.

It is, moreover, this spirit that describes the essence of Imani Temple, which is affectionately known as the "Faith House where the wounded are truly welcome and the faithful have fellowship with Christ."[6] This motto of hospitality is of particular importance because of the ecclesiastical baggage that many Imani members brought. Many, like Mo, did not grow up in the church and found themselves on a journey seeking something new as young adults and a way to find ultimate meaning in their lives. Initial experiences of "church hurts"[7] left them cautious and on guard against religion, preachers, and hypocritical members.

Imani provided them with a safe space to heal and find wholeness. Some found Imani on the pilgrimage from church to church following years of absence from organized religion. Kennon Mitchell, for example, considered himself "spiritual but not Christian," before coming to Imani. Influenced by his study of Kemetic religion, he said, "I rejected most preachers because their historical orientation was off." He and others like him abandoned religion more generally in search of a meaning and belonging found exclusively in their cultural roots.

For this group, Imani provided a classroom to learn through worship, fellowship, and service, as well as an important link between faith and culture and a foundation for a strong Christian identity. Still others joined who were raised in the church but adamantly swore they would never set foot in a church again once they became adult. But their movement toward middle age caused them to rethink that declaration. Imani provided for them an extended family environment that embraced all and defined family in terms of its function as an African village rather than its form as defined in terms of society. But for all, there was something about the Faith House that encouraged a sense of Collective Work/Responsibility and inspired a movement toward Creativity through spiritual restoration.

This congregation now claims 380 on its rolls, with about 150 active members, close to two-thirds of which are under the age of forty. Interestingly, only about twenty of the 380 members live in Pomona, which is a predominately Latino/a community. Most of the others reside in the surrounding suburbs and travel between twenty-five to thirty miles one way each Sunday and at least one additional evening during the week, as they participate in their chosen ministries. It is because of this reality that the members of Imani Temple rely on the strength of its extended-family bond and the functionality of an African village to sustain and empower them. For the majority of the Imani congregation, who must also travel into Los Angeles each day for work, their home neighborhoods often resemble communities of strangers, where they know their neighbors casually but not on any intimate or trusting level—"bedroom communities" where the demands of a daily commute into the city leave little time for anything but sleeping. If there are any possibilities for building a sense of community in these neighborhoods, they are drastically limited by the realities of the daily commute. Additionally, the diverse racial/ethnic makeup of these areas create less of a chance for connections around a common cultural heritage. But Imani members experience an alternative community that finds strength in its cultural connection and empowerment in its faith commitment.

For a full appreciation of how and why Collective Work/Responsibility and Creativity, centered on collaboration and restoration, are such vital parts of the Imani experience, it is important to get a clear sense of the larger history and ethos of African American life in southern California. This is a story of movement and change that has shaped a regional identity and established specific values. While many of Imani's members were born in California, their parents and grandparents were, for the most part, involved in one of several major migrations of African Americans within the United States. The most notable, the "Great Migration," is characterized by historian Milton Sernett as the "Second Emancipation" when African Americans "escaped" to the

North in "waves of varying intensity between 1915 and1940,"[8] as they sought freedom and opportunity not available in the South. This rural-to-urban migration filled northern and eastern cities like Chicago, Baltimore, and Detroit with families in search of the promised land. But prior to this more celebrated move, there was another equally significant migration of African Americans to various parts of the West. Migrants known as the Exodusters initiated a rural-to-rural relocation following the failure of Reconstruction in 1877 as they sought freedom and opportunity in land acquisition, differing from their northern counterparts who would later search for urban jobs.[9]

They paved the way for a slow but steady stream of African Americans moving westward throughout the mid-twentieth century, making their homes in the cities of Seattle, Portland, San Francisco, Oakland, Los Angeles, and San Diego. They accounted for 70 percent of the black population in that area of the west by the 1990s.[10] Since the early 1990s, a region east of Los Angeles known as the Inland Empire has become the fastest growing area in southern California. The counties of Riverside and San Bernadino, where most of the Imani members live, have grown steadily due to a constant flow of households leaving the Los Angeles metropolitan area.[11]

In these parts of the Inland Empire, some have found affordable housing, better schools, lower crime, and efficient freeway systems, but for far too many others there is still poverty, crime, insufficient social and health resources, and poor education. In the early years of the twenty-first century, therefore, the continued legacy of African American migration and settlement in the West continues in the migratory patterns within southern California. Like their forebears of the nineteenth and early twentieth centuries, these families seek better opportunities, less violence, and a higher quality of life.

Another important factor characteristic of the region is the increasing racial/ethnic diversity. Because of the steady growth of the Latino/a population and an increase in the presence of Asian/Pacific islanders since the 1990s, there is no longer any one racial group that is the majority.[12] Moreover, the formation of community around cultural specificity is less of a common experience than it is in the more ethnically and racially restricted cities of the Midwest and the East. It leaves the members of Imani in search of an extended family experience where they can embrace spiritual restoration and a collaborative communality that resemble Creativity and Collective Work/Responsibility.

During their short life as a southern California congregation seeking community, Imani has met with misunderstandings and has been mislabeled as non-Christian. The churches in the immediate community, for example, cordially welcomed Imani as neighbors when they first arrived. Subsequent efforts toward fellowship, however, were more difficult because of different beliefs about the need to combine Christian faith and African culture. Even the name Imani Temple *Christian* Fellowship was not enough to convince these congregations that they shared the same gospel message.

A similar experience emerged within the early Imani membership that resulted in several "painful exoduses" by members who had negative notions of what it means to embrace an African identity. Despite these challenges, the members of Imani view themselves as a "faithful, Bible-believing church."[13] They claim the Apostles Creed and affirm the Bible as the "verbally inspired Word of God" and the "infallible, authoritative rule of faith and conduct."[14] They also embrace an evangelical spirit that mandates, in their mission statement, that they be "a dynamic spiritual organism, empowered by the Holy Spirit to share Christ with as many people as possible through our fellowship, culture and community activities."[15]

This community of faith seeks ways to live their doctrinal position and theological convictions in conjunction with their African culture that finds its most obvious experience through a communal spirit. Despite the fact that some Imani members have congregational experiences in other denominations, this community of faith consciously claims no ecclesiastical affiliation. "The challenge of deciding on one denomination," recalled Kafela, "was to run the risk of splitting the church because of the variety of traditions we represent." But a more telling reason was that a common culture rather than a common religious tradition was a more attractive point of unity for this pastor and his youthful congregation.

Claiming denominational independence eliminates, for them, any doctrinal or theological constraints that may be imposed by an ecclesial body, but it also provides the freedom to be more intentional in the development of the congregational identity and commitment. It is important to note that Imani is not antidenomination as much as they are pro-culture. Kafela strongly believes that an emphasis on congregational unity around culture is more relevant in the development of the twenty-first-century church because of escalating levels of cultural diversity and the increasing emphasis on identity shifts and clarifications due to post-modern decentering and recentering. But another key part of the culture that impacts Imani, given its youthful makeup, is the hip-hop culture.

"In order to have a truly evangelistic mission that serves the lost of this generation," said Kafela, "the witness of the gospel must extend beyond traditional boundaries." With that in mind, he and Imani have allowed their connection to African culture to partner with the reality of hip-hop and their commitment to the Christian gospel. This posture essentially lessens the need for a link with a traditional religious body and increases the possibility of freedom to express the multiple aspects of their culture within a Christian context.

Their doctrinal and theological statements are not unlike other congregations with a more conservative conviction. Throughout their church documents is found the language of conversion and covenant and the mandate to be saved in order to serve. There is, however, another dimension to their quest for redemption and sanctification that looks to the Holy Spirit as the source that restores and renews. This belief envisions a Creativity that restores and reclaims both authentically cultural and spiritual voices. It is through this twofold utterance that Imani understands and accepts their commitment to share "Christ, Culture and Community," with all who so desire. It is, consequently, through an independent, nondenominational posture that Imani believes they can best live out this understanding of the gospel without denominational or bureaucratic hindrances.

Although Imani's independent status leaves them at a disadvantage in terms of more formal denominational connections and networks, this congregation has discovered ways to find additional fellowship as well as support for their work of ministry. Imani is one of twenty-six churches in the Inland Empire who make up the Congregations Organized for Prophetic Engagement (COPE), and Kafela serves as its president. The pastors and members in these small- to medium-sized congregations work with civic and parachurch organizations to collaboratively develop strategies that will revitalize their communities and empower their members. Organized under the larger umbrella of the Los Angeles Metropolitan Churches (LAM), COPE and its affiliate, United African American Ministerial Action Council (UAAMAC) are committed to playing a key role in policy-making and community revitalization in their local areas.[16] In the spirit of both Collective Work/Responsibility and Creativity, Imani in conjunction with COPE is actively involved in a number of initiatives to restore and revitalize the African American communities in the Inland Empire.

The Executive Director of LAM, Rev. Eugene Williams, Pastor Kafela, and representative members of COPE, for example, met with the district attorney and public defender of the San Bernadino County probation department to map out strategies for implementing the newly adopted Literacy/GED Initiative Program.[17] This program "mandated a five-year pilot program that authorized judges to sentence low-level offenders and probationers to literacy or high school equivalency programs."[18] It came after three years of meeting with the Los Angeles district attorney's office and elected officials as well as prayer vigils and letter-writing campaigns within the LAM associated congregations.[19] It resulted in former Governor Pete Wilson's signature and support of Assembly Bill 743 that essentially authorized the sentencing of nonviolent offenders to *school*, not *jail*. The program will be considered successful if 10 percent get their GED within three years. In a time when 23 percent[20] of all parolees in the state return to the communities of the Inland Empire, this legislation came as an act of both Collective Work/Responsibility and Creativity—a collaborative use of human resources in a spirit of restoration and revitalization.

Another LAM initiative that takes a prominent place in the life of Imani is the "One Church, One School Initiative."[21] The basic strategy is to link churches, neighborhoods, and schools in ways that will maximize both people and community resources. The expectation is to involve parents, church members, clergy, and teachers and school administration in the creation of a learning environment that will assist students with academic skills and to cultivate a love of learning. The school adopted by Imani is the Frisbee Middle School, located in Rialto, about fifteen miles southwest of Pomona. Located in the area of the Inland Empire with the lowest achievement records, this school is making tremendous advances under the leadership of a young principal, Kennon Mitchell, who is also an Imani member.[22]

The story of this school's challenges and achievements can be appreciated most fully in the context, once again, of African American life in southern California. "The community of Rialto is populated by 60 percent Latino/a, 35 percent African American, 1 percent Asian American, and less than 5 percent European American," said Mitchell. "While a few single family homes are found throughout," he continued, "the majority of its residents live in housing projects, apartments, and trailer parks. There is additionally a number of group homes that house children and youth in foster care." The student body of Frisbee reflects the larger demographics with the median family income of less than $17,500 per year. As a result of California legislation, the school receives $90,000 annually to provide bilingual education and support for its second language students.[23] In recent years, this has resulted in marked academic progress among Latino/a students because of the efforts to create and maintain a culturally relevant environment. The story of their African American counterparts, however, is not as impressive, but in a spirit of Creativity, efforts are made to restore, renew, and revitalize the learning experience and environment for these youth.

This reality presented a special challenge for Mitchell as principal. In addition to his responsibilities for curriculum development and teacher training and support, he searched for ways to reverse the cycle of failure and encourage academic excellence for African American students. An important part of this program was to identify and train teachers who possessed the ability, sensitivity, and willingness to try a new thing. Both interview and observation protocols were used to select teachers from the existing Frisbee staff who would work best. They then received guidance on the best learning and teaching styles and techniques for the African American students. In an after-school format, two days per week, these youth began to receive some of the assistance they so desperately needed. While both boys and girls participated equally in the academic sessions, male and female mentors were enlisted to provide gender specific coaching and nurturing. "It was in this phase of the program," said Mitchell, "that I took special interest in African American boys and solicited help from the men of Imani."

His quest began by seeking out African American boys within the school with less than 1.0 GPAs. These young males did not qualify for federal dollars, as did their Latino counterparts. This committed educator, however, used supporting data that showed African American males were at risk and required specific intervention[24] to craft a male mentoring program called MAAT. Mitchell also instituted a female program called Sankofa to address the needs of African American adolescent girls as the second lowest achieving subgroup in the California school system. "In both cases," he said, "the youth were quite capable of academic success; however, they were challenged with low self-esteem, low-expectation, and limited or poor role models and required more intentional academic support and social nurturing." Through joint field trips and lessons on African American history, the boys and girls are provided with experiences that enhance their academic curriculum. In separate gender based sessions[25] they experience much-needed mentoring and modeling. The girls are encouraged to discover themselves and engage in dialogue that enhances self-esteem and supports positive goal-setting. The boys experience an intentionally disciplinary regimen that had consequences for the classroom in the form of more focus and attentiveness in class work and more respect for and sensitivity to other students.

The men of Imani are a key part of the experience for both boys and girls. They initiated a Rites of Passage program, modeled after their own, that required the boys to strive for completion of a portfolio that included service projects, selected readings, speaking engagements, debates, research, and role play. This all culminated in a Rites of Passage ceremony that celebrated their success and laid the foundation for their future. "In addition to academic support," said Mitchell, "the very presence of responsible men and women made all the difference in the world, teaching the boys to honor and respect women and giving the girls an opportunity to learn to interact in a healthy way with men." There were additional efforts to include parents through quarterly parent nights as well as periodic assignments that involved family members.

This partnership between Frisbee Middle School and Imani exemplified both Cooperative Work/Responsibility and Creativity as they collectively gathered to support as well as restore and revive a neglected segment of the African American community. Despite the congregation's commitment to evangelize, they were careful to recognize and honor the separation of church and state. But they also unapologetically conducted themselves as men of God as they brought both cultural and spiritual presence into the experience. "The mere presence of African American men for both the boys and girls created for some and restored for others a positive image of African American Christian manhood," commented Mitchell. "It also, on a more subtle level, affirms the importance of honoring one's faith and culture in daily life." This example of outreach viewed through the lenses of both Collective Work/Responsibility and Creativity was also seen in some of the ministries of Imani.

As with other congregations, Imani members gravitate to the ministries that enhance their gifts and support their needs. There are the traditional fellowship groups that gather men, women, youth, young adults, singles, and married couples together for fellowship.[26] Each of these ministries understands itself as only one piece of a larger puzzle that fits together, collaboratively, for the good of all. There is a place for every interest and need and there is a commitment to live as an African village where roles are clearly defined and work is done collaboratively, with individuals conscious of the impact of their work on the whole group. This communal and restorative experience is seen clearly in the work of the Imani women.

While Imani has a solid group of men in its congregation, like most churches across the nation, it is made up of strong, hard-working, spirited women who comprise over 70 percent of its membership. If one were to look at the list of the thirty-one ministries at Imani, only one would easily identify as women's ministry—"Women Seeking Christ" (WSC). Kathy Kafela, wife of the pastor, said, "It is unreal to believe that this is the only place where women's presence is found, for our leadership permeates the ministry and mission of Imani." As mentioned earlier, the earliest inspiration and support for this congregation came from two key women in Pastor Kafela's life, and the majority of the eight core members that founded this congregation were women.

The work of the WSC, moreover, is an example of Creativity. Their sole purpose is to restore their relationship with God by "seeking the Master's face" and reconnecting with their sisters "across the generations." This is a particularly significant experience because of the generational blending within this congregation. The fact that two-thirds of the women in this ministry are under the age of forty creates a distinctive challenge of balancing the perspectives, insights, needs, and desires of women in two generations. Through dialogue and discussion as well as disagreement and tears, these women confront head-on the need to restore, renew, and reconnect. With Creativity as its goal, this gathering of women, consequently, is the primary place to nurture and cultivate women leaders at Imani. It is the place where they discover ways to bring honor to those of mature years and celebrate the energy and innovation of those of more youthful experiences through Bible study, discussion, prayer, and praise.

In addition to being integral to these gatherings within the Imani family, the women are also involved in experiences of outreach and education with women in the community. On the local level, they sponsor monthly "Morning Glory" sessions for women from various churches in the Inland Empire. They gather during this time for praise, worship, and fellowship in an effort to support and network with other women in their ministry efforts. Over the past three years, they have also sponsored an annual women's conference. These three-day events feature a keynote speaker as well as a number of other sessions that speak to the challenges and promises of being "godly women." What is distinctive about each of these gatherings is that they are grounded on the belief that restoration and revitalization of the church and community will come through the prayers and presence of women. Their most recent conference has had an impact across the nation as they have begun to network with women in Ohio, North Carolina, and New York, which they hope will lead to a national conference in 2004.

The women of Imani, like the women who followed Jesus, are dynamic, gifted, anointed, and ever-ready to serve. Their presence and power is grounded in a Creativity that promises to perpetuate life and restore wholeness in Imani and the community. An important part of this restoration connects to the principle of Collective Work and Responsibility, seen in the active participation of women on the pastoral team of Imani. Shirley O'Veal, for example, serves as one of the associate pastors. This licensed minister is a mature woman who brings the gift of wise counsel and anointed guidance to the WSC ministry as well as prophetic preaching and teaching to the entire congregation. Three other younger women, Janise L. Bush, Tamika R. Casey, and Christy Robinzine are official "ministers" at Imani who provide primary leadership through preaching and teaching at the women's conferences. Their gifts also extend to the larger congregation through service in the form of church administration, sick visitation, prayer leadership, and the mentoring of children. These women consider themselves to be in process, becoming God's masterpieces, as they provide the backbone and foundation for the vital and growing ministry at Imani.

Another interesting example of this shared communality is seen in expressions of Creativity in the worship service. At Imani, along with other congregations that celebrate the black religious experience, the music is a key part of the worship experience. However, the primary attention and responsibility to make the worship "happen" at Imani is not focused on the choir, as in many other churches. The choir is an integral part of a larger ministry of worship rather than the "featured attraction" of the ministry of music. As you enter the sanctuary to worship, for example, you are met with the sound of conga drums. Of the four drummers, two are youth and one of the youth is a young girl.

The drumming varies in its volume and intensity and serves as a kind of musical prelude to worship. After the call to worship, a fifteen-to twenty-member choir rises from the first two rows, comes before the audience, and leads the congregation in two or three inspiring and spirit-filled songs, made up of contemporary gospel and "rap." The ministry of music also includes a guitar and an electric piano that are played passionately and improvisationally during interludes in the worship. A contemporary poem is read just before the scripture, creatively linking the Word of the past with words of the present. Just before the sermon, when it is customary in African American churches to have a selection from the choir, the praise dancers worship through movement. "The inspired movement just before the spoken Word," explained Kafela, " is a concrete example of the embodiment of God's Word and gives me great inspiration for my preaching through this creative form in worship." In their worship and ministries, Imani attempts to live in the communality of an African village. Looking through the lenses of Collective Work/Responsibility and Creativity, we see a means to enhance mutuality and encourage restoration.

Ritual is an important way to reinforce meaning and identity in a communal context. In addition to the ritual celebrations that are experienced in the more traditional sense (for example, communion and baptism), baby dedication has become an important part of the congregational process at Imani. Because the congregation affirm that baptism is an outward sign of an inward conviction, they perform the rite on persons who verbally profess their faith in Christ, even children. Infants who are unable to make that profession are dedicated and the ritual becomes a celebration of a new life as a gift of hope and the promise of God's continued presence in the community of faith. At the dedication of baby boy Amari Osonduagwuike, the congregation experienced an expression of that hope. It began with the beating of drums that symbolically pronounced the gathering of those present with the ancestors.

Throughout the ritual there is dance, the pouring of libations as well as prayers, but the high point is the affirmation expressed by the community on behalf of the child and family. There is also a point when the male or female members of the community (depending on whether a girl or boy is being dedicated) come to the father or mother, one by one and whisper a word of encouragement and affirmation into the parent's ear. When asked about the impact of this experience on her understanding of her role as mother and a member of the community, Danielle Osonduagwuike said, "This experience shows that being a parent is not to be taken lightly. It emphasizes the spiritual connection between the family and the community as it brings the child into the village." Baby dedication is the point of entry for many children in the Imani family. It opens the way for their presence and participation in a number of youth ministries that are emerging as this small but vibrant church grows.

At Imani, there is also a conscious effort to encourage and support a shared leadership model that discourages "kingdom building" in the church and moves toward more of a communally based leadership model. An example is seen in the work of the Council of Elders. This seven-member group, appointed by the pastor,[27] seeks to "support and facilitate the pastor's vision, and as such are deeply committed to the task of organizing, equipping and leading a spiritually disciplined flock of God's people in service to the vision of Imani and the ministry of Jesus Christ."[28] The term "elder" is used more figuratively than literally in this context because of the youthful makeup of the congregation. There are, for example, "elders" that are as young as thirty years old who share equally with those in their mid–fifties. Together they form a Council that combines youthful energies with more seasoned experiences of life.

During a monthly meeting of the Council, for example, a written agenda was distributed but there was a more pressing concern for consideration.[29] On the previous Sunday, the members had arrived at the church to find gang graffiti defacing their building; two days later, the phone lines were cut. After a review of the events and the facts, the floor was opened for a suggested strategy on how to deal with the "attacks." A lively discussion included suggestions for both protection from the gang and engagement with them. Then someone pointed out that although Imani had been in the community since 1999, it essentially had entered someone else's "village" without official attempts outside of the local churches to connect with others in the community. The members of the Council then recognized that the concern Imani had for the respect of its "sacred space" was also an equally important concern for those who lived in that community, especially the gang members.

The Council of Elders decided, consequently, on a multipronged approach that would begin to build the necessary relationships with the gangs in the community and open the way for ongoing Collective Work/Responsibility among all involved. Throughout this process the chair and the pastor shared the role of facilitator, asking for points of clarification and navigating the discussion without interjecting specific perspectives. It is important to note that the consensus did not come easily. Some members clearly "shared" the leadership more than others and the ideal of a shared approach emerged slowly amid obvious tension around the process. Nevertheless, this is an example of the challenges and issues that Imani must face as it attempts to creatively approach problem-solving from a communal, shared leadership model as seen through the lens of Collective Work/Responsibility.

Ironically, the desire of the Council to view their presence in the Pomona community as members of an African village was only prompted after an attack on its property. The insight of the Council member regarding Imani's unofficial entrance in the community becomes more emphatic given the fact that there are three churches within a one-block radius—one immediately across the street. Surely their joint efforts could provide a strong Christian presence in the community and lessen these kinds of attacks. This is a part of the complicating reality of community life for the members of Imani, particularly because of the challenges of their "commuter church" lifestyle. What may seem to be a clear disconnect between their "talk" of being an African village and their "walk" within the immediate Pomona community is in reality the result of misunderstanding and rejection spoken of earlier, based on misinterpretations of how one can be at once African and Christian.

Congregations, as described earlier by Hopewell, are indeed bound together by more than creeds, polity, and programs and possess distinctive languages through their stories, rituals, and symbols. This narrative portrait of Imani Temple paints a picture of the birth and early growth of a new congregation. In it we see the creation of images and symbols that will define meaning and belonging and support values of Creativity and Collective Work and Responsibility. They will also sustain this African American congregation that finds itself in the midst of an ethos of seeking and searching in the early twenty-first century. Their story reveals a response to the need to creatively restore a sense of wholeness for a people who have been fragmented geographically as well as spiritually. Their story also tells of their efforts to establish the contours of a communal experience that shares collectively in their work and responsibility. As a collective narrative, Imani's story provides us with a glimpse of both the promise and the challenge of what it means to walk the talk and keep the faith.

WALKIN' THE TALK OF CREATIVITY AND COLLECTIVE WORK/RESPONSIBILITY
Creativity

The word "creativity" in the minds of many usually causes one to think of artistic ability in a variety of forms such as dance, music, and art. This understanding is not foreign to the members of Imani or the residents of Los Angeles and the surrounding Inland Empire. Karenga's commitment to "leave our community more beautiful and beneficial than we inherited it" has a haunting significance in light of the challenges of rebuilding Los Angeles following the riots of 1992. The acquittal of four L.A. police officers, despite a video showing graphic detail of the beating of Rodney King, was the spark that ignited several days of riots.[30] Ten years later there are signs of revitalization as some attempt to live out Karenga's description of Creativity. Several prominent sports figures,[31] for example, provided financial backing for a number of businesses in an attempt at restoring beauty and providing certain benefits for the community. But these efforts were made in the presence of what some call "bureaucratic slights, missteps, and blind spots" that impeded more genuine revitalization by the city. This contributed to the ongoing feelings of "black malcontent," poverty, and unemployment that provided the kindling for the riots in the first place.[32] The real revitalization and Creativity needed here goes beyond new buildings, beautiful land-scaping, and thriving businesses and speak to the deeper need for a re-newal of the spirit. The members of Imani are familiar with this longing. Even though most of them have migrated from L.A. and only commute in for work, they are ever conscious of the need for a dimension of Creativity that impacts the inward life at the core of the spirit.

For Karenga, Creativity is an "original act" that is seen as a move-ment to "push back the currents of chaos and decay"[33] and acknowl-edges African spirituality as the source of power and purpose. It is also described as both a restorative and progressive act that moves from a state of chaos and fragmentation to completion and wholeness. The ability to do so, for him, is based on the belief that Creativity is an in-nate part of the human spirit and its use revitalizes the human capacity for "cultural restoration and renewal."[34] The challenge, nevertheless, of a restorative and progressive perfection is that perfection by its very nature is often an illusive and unattainable goal. The word defined means "completion; without fault or defect." Such a difficult and even unreal-istic goal can lead one to be driven to desire to eliminate all deficien-cies, can become a means to an end, and may encourage the kind of competition and comparison that is fatal to cohesion in community.

Clearly the most obvious examples of Creativity at Imani are found in ministries of dance, music, and poetry in worship. It extends further to include other innovative ministries that serve to revitalize the com-munity for greater work and services. In this congregation, however, these creative expressions are linked more closely to the divine plan and purpose of a Creator God than the innate ability and capacity of hu-manity. The placement of dance just before the preached word and po-etry just before the reading of the scripture, for example, point to cre-ative expression that finds its locus in the vitality and dynamism of the Holy Spirit. While each require some level of human skill and preci-sion, the final execution is credited to the work of the Spirit. This pres-ence that comes forth in song and dance as well as teaching and preach-ing is understood as human expression of the divine reality that empowers and sustains the body of Christ. Moreover, the capacity for renewal and restoration begins with the creative power of God.

Within the story of Imani, moreover, Creativity takes on a different focus when seen through the lens of the restated definition: *to ground our creative energy in a renewed and renewing relationship with God that restores our African American communities and creates new possibilities for commitment to the Diaspora and the world for the good of all people.* With this as a backdrop, restorative and progressive *perfection* becomes an experience of restorative and progressive *excellence*. Defined as the quality of being "outstandingly good of its own kind," to be excellent suggests that there are many levels of attainment according to "its own kind."

To restore people to a place of excellence means that whatever one brings, as fragmented as it may be in reality, it is complete in the eyes of God. Any genuine effort, therefore, toward progressively cultivating that excellence is in itself the success. These small but significant successes, for instance, were experienced by Imani members through the support of a community that affirmed them in their brokenness and encouraged them toward healing. In the Faith House where the "wounded are truly welcomed and the faithful have fellowship with Christ," restorative and progressive *perfection* was clearly not the goal. However, a restorative and progressive *excellence* that finds goodness in "its kind," opened the door for a Creativity that transcends mere aesthetic expression.

This excellence is closely connected to the "Creative soul force" defined by Carlyle F. Stewart III that provides the "cultural mechanisms that enable African Americans to adapt, transform, and transcend reality through the creative construction of black culture."[35] It is a Creativity that gives them the freedom to see themselves as God sees them and then be empowered to engage in restorative and progressive excellence for the good of the community. When faith is added to culture, moreover, the ability to attain and maintain excellence is not based on the human capacity of self-mastery but on the empowerment of God through the Holy Spirit. For Imani it outlines the contours of an African-centered spirituality that acknowledges the cosmological foundations of an African worldview, yet lives it out in the realities and challenges of being Christian in an American context.

Collective Work/Responsibility

This principle at first glance is very basic. It expresses the need for people to work with collaboration and accountability in all areas of life. In a congregational context, this is of particular importance because of the voluntary nature of church work. There is no monetary compensation for church service, so motivation must come through a sense of collective ownership and individual satisfaction. This experience of Collective Work/Responsibility was common at Imani, primarily because of the newness of the church. When people joined, they were not attracted by a beautifully adorned building or a spirit-filled choir but by a more subtle yet profound vision of what this congregation could become. Once this vision was embraced, a commitment to Collective Work/Responsibility easily followed that aligned with the new definition: *to build and maintain our communities as Africans in Diaspora who live in a context of service and mutual accountability in America and the world, strengthened by the liberating spirit of God.* This kind of commitment in the early stages of Imani's growth was essential because of the decision to be an independent church. There were no denominational committees to support the emerging leadership or ecclesial funds to sponsor new ministries, so the need to work collaboratively and to be accountable was imperative. It is important to note that Imani's commitment to be independent does not mean that they are "Lone-Ranger Christians." The ecumenical connections that they established through their involvement with COPE, through the local and national networking of the women, as well as their continued experiences of worship and fellowship and even modest financial support to other congregations, expanded their efforts toward Collective Work/Responsibility.

Another important factor that has an impact on Imani's passion to embrace a communal, collaborative, and cooperative relationship is seen in its generational makeup. As mentioned earlier, over 50 percent of the membership is under forty years old, placing them in the category of "generation X." While some sociologists identify this group chronologically as those born between the mid-1960s and the early 1980s,[36] Tom Beadoin suggests that it be classified more closely with the popular culture that shapes it.[37] This generation of latch-key kids bore the brunt of escalating divorce rates, out-of-wedlock births, and absent fathers more than the previous generation.[38] Gen-Xers are highly individualistic yet they tend to "yearn for religious community and for the support and nurture that can come from the presence of others who share similar commitments," unlike their baby-boomer parents.[39] Their desire for community may not guarantee an equally strong commitment to responsibility but the generational legacy that they bring to Imani combined with the realities of a commuter lifestyle in southern California provide a crucible of care and concern from which a passionate sense of community can emerge.

Imani's experience then is very similar to Karenga's notion of Collective Work/Responsibility, which is "committed to active and informed togetherness on matters of common interest."[40] This commitment also recognizes that true liberation and progress will not take place without an emphasis on active cooperation. Karenga continues to point out that the result of such collaborative and accountable involvement is freedom, but that freedom can never be appreciated unless all Africans are free. Imani would agree with the need for liberation from various forms of social oppression but their focus centers more locally on African Americans and their strivings toward full potential. Their works, mentioned earlier, with the educational initiatives in the African American communities of southern California are a testimony to that fact.

This discussion of Collective Work/Responsibility, with an emphasis on social change to "solve" the problems of our sisters and brothers, reveals two different loci of power. For Karenga it is in the capacity for human self-mastery in imitation of the Creator. This is based on a humanism that "begins with commitment to and concern for the humans among whom we live and to whom we owe our existence, i.e., our own people."[41] This form of humanism begins with the spiritual tradition of Africa that affirms the positiveness of creation, which leads to a belief in the goodness and potential of humanity. Combined with the indivisible nature of African freedom, this principle recognizes the necessity and the responsibility for self-correction.

If, for example, an action or directive is not for the good of all, the spirit of Collective Work/Responsibility mandates a self-critique that brings all things into communal alignment. This definitive trust in the human capacity to provide such an analysis is not the position taken, however, by Imani. Where Karenga's reliance in the power and presence of the Creator is implicit, leaving human capacity in the forefront, Imani stresses the liberating strength of Christ that empowers in the midst of human finitude.

It is through the lens of the new definition of Collective Work/Responsibility that we see Imani's attempt at adding African culture to their faith commitment as they prepare for ministry and service. Imani's mission emphases on renewal and revival are grounded in a belief in the resurrection power of Christ. As essential as it is for this congregation to engage in evangelism and outreach, however, they recognize that their first task is to renew and maintain a solid relationship with Christ as the source of their strength. They do not deny the potential for human action but, unlike Karenga, they downplay and even discourage visions of self-mastery and rely instead on the directives from the Master. In their attempt to engage in a shared leadership model that resembles an African village, there is always the need for self-critique and self-correction. But because their notion of self acknowledges both sin and righteousness, they are compelled to rely on the admonishment and correction of God that comes through prayer and the prophetic Word. Both Karenga and Imani are committed to a kind of "communitarian social order,"[42] that supports Collective Work/Responsibility and draws on the resources of an African worldview and culture; but where Karenga partners ancient Egyptian culture with faith in human potential, Imani attempts to marry an African-centered spirituality with a Christ-rooted ministry.

Some sociologists would classify Imani as a congregation that has several post-traditional characteristics. While Imani is not a megachurch, as most are, it shares some traits, including a theological conservatism without being fundamentalist, no formal denominational ties, strong lay leadership through the use of spiritual gifts, worship and ministry intentionally designed for a specific audience, and a commitment to leading constituents to a life of discipleship.[43] Scholars also point out that because of Imani's nondenominational status it is not a bearer of an inherited tradition.[44] They ask questions like, "How can it go in neglect of an inherited tradition without losing its Christian identity? How can the congregation dance with the culture without allowing the culture to write the music?" It is precisely *because* Imani embraces the "music" of an African-centered spirituality that it is able to live into the renewed notion of Collective Work/Responsibility that combines faith and culture and maintain its sense of community. This is because the African-centered culture is void of a sacred/secular dichotomy and brings a more holistic worldview that encourages a spirit of Collective Work/Responsibility. In many ways, Imani *is* the bearer of an inherited tradition—an African-centered spiritual tradition—that has sustained countless generations of African descent in America and continues to empower and transform congregational life into the twenty-first century.

three

First Afrikan Presbyterian Church

Self-Determination and Cooperative Economics

THE CONGREGATIONAL STORY

The year is 2022. The place is Lithonia, Georgia. The event is the First Afrikan Annual Consortium. The chairperson rises to the podium, calls the meeting to order, and invites the participants to join in the institutional affirmation:

> The First Afrikan Consortium is an Africentric Christian Ministry that empowers women, men, youth, and children to move from membership to leadership in the church, community and world.[1]

The audience responds in unison with a joyful and hearty "Axe" (pronounced ah-sheh´)[2] as they take their seats. Then spokespersons from the various collaborative bodies give brief highlights from their annual reports before the assembly begins its more formal proceedings. The first report comes from Bishop Emeritus Dr. Mark A. Lomax, who gives an account of the growth and progress of First Afrikan churches. "I am happy to report," he begins, "that to date, the total membership in our six congregations located in Atlanta; Lithonia; Ghana, West Africa; Chicago; Los Angeles; and Philadelphia is now 64,500 members." He goes on to state that together they share a $2.1 billion annual budget with $35 billion in endowments. Next there is a report of the Black Kabbalah Institute, given by Dr. Will Coleman. This international think tank on traditional Afrikan spiritual disciplines has over 255,000 disciples worldwide with $20 billion in endowments. Dr. Coleman reports, "In recent months we have finally added to our many publications the *African Liberation Version* of the Bible. It is now available to our Kabbalah students in Lithonia, New York, and Los Angeles as well as Tibet, Senegal, Germany, and Haiti." Then attorney Deborah Jackson, representing the First Afrikan Community Development Corporation, rises to the podium. "This has been a busy year," she begins. "Our success in resurrecting Morris Brown College many years ago has now blossomed into a student population of twenty thousand with $200 million in available scholarships." She also reports the establishment of a sacred shrine at the slave dungeons of Cape Coast in remembrance of the struggle of African peoples who were captives of the Atlantic slave trade.

This report was followed by remarks from the Uhuru Community Care Center, given by Dr. Teresa Snorton. "Our five-building complex has continued to provide social services, legal assistance, and pastoral, child, health, and hospice care throughout the years," she says "and our projected budget for the coming year is $1.7 billion." She adds further that a new property has been purchased in St. Simon Island, Georgia, and it will become a retreat center called "First Afrikan by the Sea." Finally, there is a report from the Kilombo Pan Afrikan Institute, which has a full university campus that includes kindergarten through twelfth grade as well as a theological seminary. "I am proud to announce," says Aminata Umoja, "that at long last we have been successful in establishing the First Afrikan Accreditation Association for African-centered educational institutions. This institute," she notes further, "has a $300 billion endowment and a projected budget of $30 billion in the coming year." These reports are followed by more applause and resounding shouts of "Axe," as the audience rises and joins in the singing of their theme song, "Building Beyond Our Years."

Come on and be a part of the vision, come on and be a part of the mission.
God has great plans for us, God has his hand on us.
Open your ears to take a listen, open your eye to catch the vision.
We're building a heritage with stones of righteousness;
With Christ our cornerstone, we know we're not alone;
Lending a helping hand to help us understand.
We are building far beyond our years, we are building far beyond our years.[3]

This description of the future is not a playful exercise in narrative fiction but an imaginative version of the actual notes from a visioning session of the youth of First Afrikan Presbyterian Church (FAPC) at their 2002 Churchwide Retreat. In a full-day encounter the themes "Strengthening the Community," "Recognizing Your Gifts," and "Working God's Plan," were considered and these young people took a serious step toward listening to the voice of God in their midst. Behind what is seen as extremely ambitious and extravagant wishful thinking is the nascent movement of Self-Determination as well as Cooperative Economics in the hearts, minds, and spirits of the youth of First Afrikan Presbyterian Church. The first principle is evident in the bold way that they name their reality and clearly imagine themselves as subjects and not objects of history. The second principle comes alive in their emphasis on the need for monetary resources to support their vision but also in their attempt at being faithful stewards over both intellectual and spiritual "capital."

This spirit of Self-Determination and Cooperative Economics comes alive in the story of one of the youth. Ricky Stapleton[4] joined FAPC in 1994 when he was seven years old, having moved from St. Louis, Missouri, with his mother, Dorothea Williams. This family sought better opportunities in Lithonia, Georgia. Former Baptists, they were curious about a church that some friends had rejected as being "too black." While they visited other congregations, Ricky and his mother found in First Afrikan a spiritual home as well as a place of affirmation and encouragement. Ricky said, "At First Afrikan, I was introduced to Africentricity as a lifestyle." For him, this included learning more about African history and culture but also the importance of working toward economic independence in the black community.

45

In this congregation, he often heard the phrase "buy black" and observed members who displayed an entrepreneurial spirit and who expressed the need to create businesses that returned wealth back into the African American community. These examples nurtured seeds of purpose already active in the life of this little boy. Since the age of seven, for example, he earned extra money caring for lawns and working on computer graphic design projects. This was a natural progression, for he simply modeled his mother as she worked hard to begin and sustain her own small business. But at the tender age of nine and a half he boldly stepped out and started Mazoos Videography. Beginning with only the most essential equipment, Ricky videotaped birthday parties and family events. As the years passed and his skills increased, he provided video services for weddings and graduations as well as public lectures and other educational events in the larger community. The profits from these early ventures were used to purchase more sophisticated equipment. Ricky said he learned from the elders in the congregations that "if you provide the best service, people will come back."

When asked about the source of motivation for this kind of work, Ricky, now sixteen years old, stated that he was always troubled by the images portrayed in the media about the African American community, especially the youth. "The media is too negative toward black people," he said. "It tells us that black is not beautiful, but at First Afrikan we get a different message." His dream, therefore, is to provide positive images of African American people and their community through his work. Ricky's goal reflects an emphasis on the importance of Self-Determination and Cooperative Economics as he describes his vision for Mazoos. He says, "I want to teach other young people who are less fortunate how to make the best use of their God-given talents. One day I want to start a training camp that will take youth to Ghana to learn about the culture while participating in projects that create and refine video production and directing skills." As he considers attending film school as a possible option one day, he also dreams of producing movies and even starting a black TV network. In all of his endeavors, said Ricky, "My number one support is God! I pray about the smallest decisions, even buying equipment. God is the reason I do everything."

Through the lenses of Self-Determination and Cooperative Economics, this young man gives an example of a vision grounded in God that names the reality and provides the opportunities for efficient and effective use of God-given gifts in the African American community. Within a mere decade, this congregation has begun to lay the foundation for the next generation as they critically examine the challenges as well as promise of their collective future as an Africentric congregation. But it is important to recognize that there is another history that extends this congregational story back over one hundred years into a time quite different from today.

Although FAPC was chartered in 1993, it was actually a new church start that replaced the Salem Presbyterian Church, established and named by the Presbytery of Atlanta in 1875. This was during a time when the South began a slow but steady recovery from the devastation of the Civil War in the midst of a chaotic Reconstruction. In the minds of most southerners, this meant the remaking of the New South in the image of the Old, regarding the relationships between their black and white constituents. Clearly the ratification of the Thirteenth, Fourteenth, and Fifteenth Amendments that abolished slavery, clarified citizenship, and gave equal protections under the law and granted the right to vote to African American males further frustrated southerners in light of a leadership shift that thrust freedmen into major political positions. But this frustration was short-lived because the end of Reconstruction in 1877 signaled the withdrawal of troops from the South, and thus an end to federal protection for African Americans and the reestablishment of white supremacy through explicit forms of segregation.

The churches of the South were not immune to this reality, as seen in the attitudes and actions of the Presbyterian Churches of the Confederate States of America in the years immediately following the war. While the freedom of African Americans was accepted as a fact of history, efforts were made by this institution to "elevate the black race in our midst to the scale of Christianity and civilization." This was the result of the general belief in the southern churches that slavery had never been a sin and had actually been in the best interest of the nation.[5] Southern Christians in general were convinced that the freedmen/women were unprepared and inherently incapable of handling their new freedom because of their obvious social, intellectual, and moral inferiority. In the Presbyterian churches this carried heavy overtones of paternalism toward African Americans that affirmed their need for help and saw that help in the form of segregated and dependent congregations.[6]

This attitude led to heated debates about the level of autonomy to be given to these churches without disturbing the traditions of power and authority that had reigned during slavery. In the midst of this discussion, an increasing number of African Americans left the Presbyterian Church for more inclusive experiences in northern Presbyterian churches or among the Methodists and Baptists.[7] But a smaller number of black church leaders, like those in North Carolina, for example, agreed to be under a white pastor if they could have their own elders and deacons. This request for a semblance of Self-Determination was troubling to most Presbyterian leaders. It meant that these African American elders and deacons, according to Presbyterian polity, would be admitted to higher courts of ecclesial law and would receive voice and vote on issues of the larger church.[8] This solution was complicated further by the fear that giving black presbyters rights equal to their white counterparts in Presbyterian governance seriously endangered the balance of power needed to maintain white supremacy.[9] A solution was reluctantly reached that allowed the formation of African American churches to be governed by their own ruling elders with the goal of later forming their own presbyteries and synods. This developed into the formation of four segregated and independent synods in the South.[10]

With this historic backdrop of the development of Presbyterianism in the South by 1875, it follows that Salem was within the tradition of Euro-American congregations in that region that did not have a goal of an integrated membership. Throughout the first half of the twentieth century, church records portrayed Salem as a congregation that had "never recruited a large membership," but "from its membership have gone useful members to bless the churches of the larger community," many of whom were graduates of Columbia Theological Seminary in Atlanta.[11] As the decade of the 1950s unfolded, Salem anticipated a better day because of the positive signs of development and expansion of the Greater Atlanta area. But little did this congregation know that these changes would drastically change the demographics and hence the racial makeup of Atlanta, DeKalb County, and Salem Presbyterian Church.

During the 1960s, the city of Atlanta began to establish a regional dominance that led to its recognition as the "Mecca of the southeast" by the 1990s. Throughout those decades, it became a major center for federal communications and transportation. Through a surge of in-migration, says Robert Bullard, the 1970s and '80s "were characterized as a time during which the city became increasingly black."[12] It was in this environment of growth and change that Salem's demographics began to reflect the larger metropolitan shift, as witnessed by Laura Durojaiye, a new African American member. "When I first came to Salem in about 1983," she recalled, "it had a white minister who provided leadership to a congregation that was approximately 70 percent white and 30 percent black, including a number of biracial couples."[13] She also remembers a brief time when there was an effort to have a co-pastorate of a white woman and a black man. Unfortunately the "white flight" that so often occurs across the nation when people of color move into a white community took its toll on the membership of Salem. By the early 1990s it was apparent that this congregation was on its deathbed. This population shift resulted in a "suburban sprawl" that greatly filled the counties of the Metropolitan Atlanta area with African American families.[14] With the promise of growth in DeKalb County, a new congregation among the growing African American population in Lithonia became an attractive possibility to the Presbytery of Greater Atlanta. So in 1991, the denomination officially dissolved Salem only to reinstate it as a new church development in 1993 called "New Salem."

As a part of the committee that dissolved the old congregation, Durojaiye recalled the rapid "bail out" that occurred as the Euro-American members of Salem became less comfortable with the new direction the Presbytery took regarding the future of the congregation. She remembers that "only eight [black] families and one white woman (who later retired and moved out-of-state) remained and formed the core for this new congregation" that was inherited by the newly selected pastor, Rev. Dr. Mark A. Lomax.

Rev. Lomax came to New Salem on a path that took him from being a member of the Church of God as a youth to being the leader of Presbyterian Church as an ordained minister. "Being raised in the Church of God," he recalls, "I could never really accept salvation as they were proposing it even as a child, because it was a very sin-oriented presentation; full of do's and don'ts, restricting my ability to really live."[15] Despite this critique of his inherited faith tradition, he remained within a theologically conservative environment throughout college as he attended Heidelberg College in Tiffin, Ohio. During that time, his efforts to find the assurance of God's grace that could give him direction in life and help him battle his personal demons led him to a month-long fast in an effort to get closer to God. "As a consequence of this discipline," he says, "I got a clear and resounding vision that I had been called to ministry, which I had until then been fighting tooth and nail." After graduation from college and relocation to Blacksburg, Virginia, this call found expression through ministry on the campus of Virginia Tech[16] as well as preaching and teaching in the United Holiness Church. It was not long, however, before he knew that more formal education was needed. He soon found a willing and resourceful mentor who arranged for a full scholarship to Trinity Evangelical Seminary in Columbus, Ohio.

During seminary, he continued ministry as assistant pastor at the Gospel Tabernacle United Holiness Church; however, its clear and adamantly anti-intellectual perspective convinced him that a denominational change was in order. What was needed was an explicit act of Self-Determination that boldly named and embraced his theological reality. So he read all he could about "every denomination in the country," aware of his opposition to the theological and bureaucratic control found in Pentecostal and Episcopal communions. Through this research he decided that the Presbyterian Church was a viable option because of its historic support of all-black judicatories in the South. He soon made the "radical switch" from Pentecostalism to Presbyterianism and took a small congregation in North Carolina as his first pastorate. He recalls that he "read everything by and for African Americans" including African, African American, Caribbean, South American, and African traditional religion, history, philosophy, and culture in an effort to try to begin to "interpret reality for African American people." After some struggle with Molefe Asante, however, he was later able to bring together a black liberation theology perspective with an African philosophy.[17]

With this new theological and cultural direction for ministry and a more explicit sense of Self-Determination, he entered his second pastorate in Atlanta, Georgia, in 1990. He experienced, however, serious resistance within a congregation that was committed to a reformed tradition and was unwilling and unable to embrace his emerging African-centered consciousness. Discouraged and dismayed after several years of conflict, he decided to leave the church in search of a more socially active ministry experience. This direction was abruptly reversed in 1993 when he reluctantly consented to be interviewed by the Greater Atlanta Presbytery for a new church start that led to his appointment as pastor of New Salem Presbyterian Church in Lithonia, Georgia. It was here that he began the next leg of his personal and professional journey with a commitment to proclaim a gospel of liberation and Self-Determination to the African American community.

April 29, 1993, was the first gathering of the newly reinstituted congregation. There were seventy-three in attendance, which netted a commitment from forty-eight to be a part of building a new church in the community. Although Lomax was clear on his theological and philosophical positions, he did not want to impose his perspectives on this new congregation. "I randomly selected twelve members who were willing to meet with me on a weekly basis to begin to envision the kind of church we wanted to build," he said. They formed a steering committee that conducted a survey in the community and compiled the findings to help determine what kind of church would meet the needs of the residents.

One of the members of the committee was Otis C. Thomas Jr.[18] This former Florida Baptist came to Lithonia with his family by way of Massachusetts. Following the lead of his wife, Sandra, they became active at Salem Presbyterian around 1985–86, and the members were very "friendly" and seemed to accept them for who they were as fellow Presbyterians. But as African Americans began to join the church the tension began to escalate. "When there were only a few of us," he recalled, "it was okay, but as more African Americans joined, whites began to move out." When the white members began to leave in larger numbers, Thomas began to wonder about the original sincerity of the church. "I had feelings of betrayal [and] I was done with church after that," he recalled. Soon, however, his disillusionment about the church changed after a conversation with the new pastor, Rev. Lomax. "I was really attracted by his whole concept about what we need to do to educate our people," he recalled. "Rather than focus on exclusion, he simply wanted to teach our people who they are. I was hooked!" This marked his return to the congregation and his excitement about serving on the new steering committee.

The brainstorming sessions of this committee and a survey conducted in the community were in addition to many casual but strategically planned conversations in parking lots and shopping centers within a five-mile radius of the church by the pastor and committee. These were attempts at gathering information that fulfilled the committee's goal "to be responsive to and proactive with the existing African American community." Another important and effective evangelical tool was open dialogue after each worship service. These sessions took place in the fellowship hall or on the church lawn, where members were invited to discuss the Sunday sermon, the weekly Bible study, or the book of the month over light refreshments. One of the unexpected outcomes of this kind of encounter was that it attracted a number of men who were impressed by the availability of the pastor to talk, dialogue, and debate openly and freely. Mr. Thomas recalled how empowering it was in those days to engage in dialogue. "Pastor Lomax would give us copies of his sermon and challenge us to 'check it out for yourself; don't take my word for it.'" It was also during this time that Thomas was encouraged to read, for the first time, a book written by an African American author. He said that it, "opened my doors and helped me understand who I was." This man who had experienced disillusionment because he felt the church had disregarded his humanity now found a level of empowerment and Self-Determination in this new congregation.

What became clear to Thomas, Durojaiye, and others on the steering committee through the survey and the conversations was that many African Americans in the area, particularly those who had recently relocated, sought spiritual as well as economic resources. They needed a message that spoke to their realities as members of middle- and upper-middle-class suburbia who were living with the promise and problems of being black in America. A relevant message for their context was particularly important because of the growing presence of prosperity ministries in their communities that was unappealing to many.[19] As this committee pondered and discussed their findings, they began a slow but sure process toward Self-Determination as they attempted to name their current reality and then prayerfully create a communal response in their renewed congregational context. The clearest sign of their emergent identity was in their efforts to rename the congregation that stated an unquestionable connection to the culture and heritage of Africa.

As stated earlier, the name "New Salem" was given to this congregation by the Presbytery as a natural progression from the founding congregation. Clearly this name, with its obvious connections to the history and ethos of colonial New England, was not descriptive in any form of the orientation or destination envisioned by this congregation. Ms. Durojaiye recalls that it became certain to those who were a part of the naming process that the word "African" must be a part of the new name. "We had fun with the name change," she said. "We knew that there was one church called First African Presbyterian Church in Philadelphia and one in Baltimore. The debate was whether or not we could call ourselves First African since there were other churches with that name." Although the name was a radical change, she said, "people probably became most squeamish about the marquis in front of the church." This visual displayed an Ankh and open Bible (turned to Ps. 68:31) superimposed on a red, black, and green image of the African continent,[20] and boldly illustrated a strong sense of Self-Determination for this new congregation.

This, along with the new name, became the motivating force behind many of the early exoduses. "We had a massive turnover," said Durojaiye, "because we had people sitting in our church who were uncomfortable because [they believed] we were too black." This accusation of being "too black" was often associated with FAPC during the early days. It was an acknowledgement, whether consciously or subconsciously, that taking the name African meant much more than embracing a geographical or historical connection. In this congregation it became a way to describe an ontological fact that affirmed who it understood itself to be. The later changing of the spelling from "African" to "Afrikan" was an attempt at making a linguistic connection, said Dr. Will Coleman, "because there are no soft sounds in African languages."[21] In the final analysis, FAPC was indeed moving in a new direction that empowered some and repelled others.

Despite the early rejections and exoduses by many that opposed or misunderstood the new Africentric focus, there were others who began to join FAPC because it was a way to connect a latent passion for African heritage with a commitment to Christian faith. This congregation, consequently, became an attractive option for the growing number of African American seminarians in the Atlanta area. Inger Anderson[22] was among several seminarians that saw it as a place to "connect faith and culture." Grace Cheptu[23] also affirmed that it helped her "reconnect culturally." They learned how to develop an African-centered ministry as they prepared for future ministry. They and many others were a part of the ministers-in-training group that began during the first few years. They met with the pastor twice a month for study and dialogue and they also took part in the development and growth of new ministries. It was also during this time that fourth Sundays became Seminarian Sunday when the ministers-in-training would have an opportunity to preach. This effort to affirm and value seminary education and to support the development of future clergy, both male and female, began during the first year at FAPC when Vanessa Gail Knight served as the first intern from 1993 to1994.

As a student at Columbia Theological Seminary, she became acquainted with FAPC when Rev. Lomax preached at one of the annual seminary events. In her effort to identify different options for her field education, she became excited about the emerging ministry, wanted to be a part of its unfolding, and soon became a student intern. "She brought excellent organizing and pastoral skills," said Lomax, "And she was a perfect complement to my personality and leadership style."

Her presence in this congregation corresponded with the early days of the steering committee as they began to flex their growing muscles of Self-Determination and envision the identity and promise of this new ministry. She was instrumental in the guidance and support of this committee as it developed mission and vision statements, grappled with a new name, and selected the first class of elders for this new congregation. Additionally, her preaching, teaching, and pastoral care provided a necessary foundation during this first year. By June of 1995 she was ordained as the first associate minister; unfortunately, she died one month later after several months of battling cancer. Her transition marked the first death of this young congregation and her absence was felt by all. In her short time at FAPC, however, she marked the starting point for an ongoing presence of seminarian support and encouragement as well as the affirmation and advancement of women in ministry in this congregation.

Between December 1993 when the official charter was issued[24] and 1997 when the congregation was able to begin to hire a full-time ministry staff, the membership grew steadily from the original forty-eight that committed in April 1993 to more than six hundred. Most of the more traditional elements of a congregation such as teaching adult Bible classes, organizing Sunday school, and performing pastoral duties were organized and implemented by the emerging group of ministers-in-training and the first class of elders. The ministries that formed and are still emerging at FAPC find their genesis in the needs and ideas of the congregation and not the pastor, extending in a real way the spirit of Self-Determination that names the reality that they live.

Worship is an important expression of this congregation's self-determined identity, and it does not resemble the more traditional Presbyterian liturgy. The order of worship printed in the weekly bulletin, for example, illustrates special emphasis and acknowledgment of the movement of the Spirit through its fourfold divisions: "Invoking God's Presence," "Inviting God's Pleasure," "Illuminating God's Word," and "Implementing God's Purpose." Throughout this movement, worship is clearly the physical embodiment of the Spirit. Following the acolytes, the procession of the choir and pastoral staff takes a back seat to the energy of liturgical dancers moving down the aisle to the beat of drums, organ, and piano. This procession as a key part of "Invoking God's Presence," says Rev. Coleman, "is a piece of our cultural and spiritual ancestry that gives a different flavor to the experience of procession and transition within the Invocation. It encourages congregational participation so that what the dancers are doing is not entertainment. It invokes," he continues, "the full, robust presence of God within the people." It is instructive to note that the pews face the chancel area, which has musical instruments on the right, a podium in the center with choir seated behind, an elevated cross, and a mud-cloth draped altar with candles and a Bible on the left. When asked about the symbolic significance of the placement of the altar, Coleman said that its location, "does not mean that the altar is insignificant but that the whole [chancel] space is an altar."

Rather than a primary focus on a single sacred object, it is an attempt to acknowledge a broader and more embodied and holistic proclamation of the gospel seen in the sacred symbols, the musical instruments, and the celebrants. "*You* are the altar," he said, "and you are the one that participates in the construction and delivery of the sermon. That's good African . . . it parallels the African notion of a participatory embodied experience with spiritual power and presence." Through worship and liturgy, then, FAPC takes a step toward Self-Determination as it names a distinctive cultural and spiritual reality in the midst of its Presbyterian heritage.

Another example of how this congregation has attempted to model Self-Determination is seen in its reappropriation of the church year. As with the traditional liturgical calendar, the church year is divided into seasons. FAPC identifies four seasons—Birth (red), Life (gold), Transformation (black), and Return (green)—as its quarterly emphases and, under these categories, "high days" are celebrated. During the first quarter, for example, the congregation observes Afrikan Liberation Month in addition to Palm Sunday, Resurrection Sunday (Easter), and Transfiguration Sunday. Next, they highlight Juneteenth along with Mother's Day and Father's Day in their springtime celebrations. The period of Transformation follows with New Afrikan Consciousness and Caribbean Liberation Month as the major focus, and finally Ancestral Remembrance Week, Zawadi Emphasis, Kwanzaa, Umoja Karamu, and Emancipation Sunday are celebrated along with Advent. Commenting on this creative innovation of tradition, Lomax said, " As we considered the basic structure of the church year as received, or should I say imposed, by Western Christendom, we began developing a calendar for the church year that we believe speaks more viscerally to African American peoples."[25]

In addition to FACP's conscious effort to integrate a more Africentric spirit in Sunday worship and year-round celebration, the language they use also reveals the important task of naming their reality. The most obvious examples are the numerous references to the presence of the ancestors and the interchangeable references to Jesus as the Black/Afrikan Messiah. It is commonplace, for example, to hear references to the ancestors during prayers and as a part of the pouring of libations in some of the rituals. Rev. Coleman explains that this is an important part of the FAPC experience referred to as the reclamation of ancestral memory. "We are learning," he says, "how to unapologetically honor and respect our ancestors as any other sane group of people do." He affirms that recapturing the memory of their African heritage for people of African descent is more beneficial to their spiritual development than emulating or imitating someone else's heritage. "But the other side [of the reclamation of ancestral memory]," he continues, "is developing a really strong prophetic vision for what our children and their children's children will believe and practice that is not culturally limited to what is commonly called the Christian faith tradition."

This acknowledgement of the ancestors is not an easy concept to grasp for some FAPC members. Freddie and Mary Young,[26] who are both retired and who were members of Salem Presbyterian Church, have varying views on the subject. While Mr. Young embraces the reclamation of ancestral memory as exciting and even empowering, he states that "the wife cannot accept the idea of meditating and talking to the ancestors." After some thought and conversation, however, she admits that, at least in theory, it is not unrelated to the way she remembers her father, who died fifty years ago. "I find myself on holidays," she begins, "wishing he was here. On his birthday I'll even say 'Happy Birthday Dad.'" While she is still a bit uncomfortable with the level of formal emphasis given to the ancestors at FAPC, she along with other members are aware of the strength one can draw from the simple act of remembering. Although she cannot fully condone the practice, she clearly does not condemn it.

On the topic of the Black Messiah, conversely, the Youngs both affirm and embrace its importance. This is despite the negative references to their blackness they experienced as children in a society of racial segregation and discrimination. "My grandmother always told us," recalled Mrs. Young, "that God is black! Anytime a person got hair like lamb's wool and feet like bronze she said he got to be black. As I got older," she continued, "I realized [that because of] where he came from, he had to be darker; he couldn't be white so what she said made sense." This belief in the African heritage of Jesus is seen in the opening section of FAPC's affirmation of faith, which is modeled after the Apostle's Creed:

> We believe that the living Creator, who was called by many powerful names in Africa and throughout the world, is not only the source of life, but also the one that sustains and liberates humanity and all of creation from the destructive powers of oppression and death. Our Redeemer was born on the peninsula of Northeast Africa as Jesus of Nazareth, the Black Messiah. He appeared among the poorest, most wretched and despised people in the Roman Empire. This African Messiah was born in a dirty manger because there was no other place for him. As our Elder Brother he grew in wisdom, knowledge and in his determination to heal the sick, raise the dead, cast out demons, and battle against all principalities and powers. Our African Messiah was arrested, tried, beaten, and lynched under the Roman Empire and with the sanction of the Jewish Sanhedrin. Our

African Messiah died and descended into the bowels of the earth. But the grave could not hold him. Our mighty African Messiah rose again, conquering the final enemy of life. Our triumphant African Messiah returned to the heavens as the king of kings and lord of lords leaving the promise of new life to all who follow the Way he himself had prepared.[27]

This affirmation of faith clearly situates Jesus geographically and historically on the continent of Africa during the time of the Roman Empire. It describes social conditions that parallel the biblical accounts of Jesus' life in a way that gives substance to his humanity. But this statement also affirms the crucifixion as well as celebrates the resurrection of a Messiah as the "King of kings and Lord of lords" who promises new life. This core belief of the gospel, although wrapped in the garment of Africentricity, is the primary reason the older members like the Youngs continue to remain at First Afrikan and to support its mission and ministry.

It is important to know that Freddie and Mary Young represent a very small part of the congregation, for nearly 80 percent of its membership is under the age of forty. The youthful makeup of this congregation, said Rev. Susan Mitchell, minister of Christian education, "is good in terms of the future because of the abundance of families with young children. But it also presents a growing edge in that these younger members are very much into their careers and families and not always as available with time to work in the ministries."[28] In addition to this reality, a far more critical one is the fact that most who joined in the early days were persons returning to church after years of absence or were first-time church members.

This presented some very interesting challenges for Christian education, said Mitchell. "We started with a large Wednesday night Bible study class for adults and Sunday school for children but because people were in different places [theologically], we created a very basic set of classes." They began with Bible Basics and Old/New Testament classes to expose them to foundational stories and characters of the Bible, then they later added theology and African spirituality, in keeping with their cultural/theological focus. "The missing link," said Mitchell "was a course on African history. This was necessary because we were talking about all this African stuff but nobody had a foundation." This new course focused on different countries and cultures and discussed them in light of their social, political, and religious contexts.

This example of an extended and intensive class content soon became the norm and each class offered at FAPC lasted one year. With this development, Mitchell recalls, "we extended our new member class to six weeks, adding information that would help new members enter the basic class at any point in the process." The need for multiple levels of Christian education to meet the challenges of a congregation with diverse religious exposure was not the only educational goal. A different one emerged that centered on the congregation's youthfulness and the need to be more relevant across generations as seen through the eyes of FAPC's first young elder, Mekeyah McQueen.

Ms. McQueen and her family joined FAPC in 1996, making this the first church home for her and her sister.[29] Because they had been introduced to African culture and values at home, the African-centered perspective at FAPC was not new but it did add to their base of knowledge. This was the case with many of the youth and children at that time, making them the first generation to grow up in this congregation. At the age of twenty-one, as a student at Spelman College, McQueen became the youngest elder chosen by the Session while simultaneously being one of the oldest youth. As an active member of the leadership of FAPC who now serves as the liaison between the youth and the Session, she detects a very different appropriation of Self-Determination between the youth and their parents. "Many adults," she said, "think that we [youth] take our African identity for granted, but because we grew up with it all around us, it has become our natural point of reference—our theological frame of reference." She observed that most adults need some level of "spiritual detox" to even begin to understand, integrate, and embrace an Africentric philosophy with Christian values. This kind of process, she believes, is not necessary for youth.

In the Bible classes, for example, she found that many of the issues were "not relevant to her because of different understandings of identity between youth and their parent's generation. She believes that teens, particularly those who grew up in FAPC, had less to "unlearn" about their faith and culture than their parents. But she added that while many youth are more knowledgeable and accepting of their African culture and Christian heritage, there is still a great challenge for the youth because they have no "fighting experience" parallel to their parents. "We have not yet had to fight," she said, "because we have no version of the civil rights or Black Power movements that caused us to flex that muscle or even see if we have that muscle to flex. Our parents are still fighting for us," she continued, "and we have not had the chance to pick up the ball." These are some of the reasons why she believes that the older generation accuses youth of acting like they have "made it" and display less of a self-determined spirit. But she cautions that despite the differences in experiences and interpretations between the generations, there must always be an acknowledgment of struggle at FAPC that keeps the gospel message on the cutting edge and balances faith with culture.

Clearly, the issue of identity and the move toward Self-Determination was a complex one. Through their efforts to take the responsibility for naming their reality and themselves as a congregation, they were challenged to create an identity broad enough to span generations as well as experiences. While some members partnered their often passionate and painful cultural experiences of the '60s and '70s with a reappropriated understanding of the gospel, others born much later combined a de facto African-centered faith with less volatile cultural experiences that required a less explicit proclamation. But there was yet another faction within the membership that adamantly believed that FAPC was not African enough.

An example was in the spring of 1996, when a group of women began to introduce conversations about some of the experiences and expression of spirituality within African traditional religions (ATR). Their conversations grew into debates, creating serious division within the church. On the one side were the women who believed that the congregational emphasis of Africentricity should lean closer to "authentic" ATR and a belief in henotheism that acknowledges a pluralism of gods.[30] On the other side were members concerned about the way this and other beliefs moved them away from the very foundation of the Christian gospel. The most vivid illustration of the seriousness of this discussion occurred one Sunday morning. During worship when the clergy processed in blue Geneva gowns rather than traditional African garb, this group of women stood in the pews with their backs to the pulpit in protest. Although the pastoral staff frequently alternated more traditional liturgical garb with African clothing in acknowledgment of and respect for the diversity of the congregation, this group interpreted their actions to be a severe compromise of the church's professed African-centered perspective. After many attempts by the pastor to reconcile this issue, including the presentation and discussion of a position paper on the matter, the members of this group withdrew their membership, leaving deep wounds. Clearly, the path toward Self-Determination at FAPC was not an easy one. They encountered two very different definitions of what it meant to be African-centered that threatened the unity and perhaps the future of the congregation.

These examples of problem and promise around the issue of identity at FAPC between 1998 and 2000 were characterized by Pastor Lomax as "years of deep struggle." It included personal challenges for the pastor as well as communal uncertainties for the members as they all struggled to comprehend what it really meant to be black and Presbyterian. This concern that haunted as well as challenged FAPC during its formative years was but a microcosm of the larger experience of many African American Presbyterians during the 1990s. In a paper written in 1993 entitled, "Is This New Wine?" prominent lay and clergy in the African American Presbyterian community grappled with this very issue. The process first of all acknowledged the identity crisis experienced by black Presbyterians, defined by Gayraud Wilmore as, "an event in the development of a person or organization when a decision must be made to either affirm or deny one's historical individuality."[31] But more importantly, it affirmed the value of an "Afrocentric" perspective that, "enables persons of African Descent to achieve from within an African center, what Jesus talked about when he articulated the great commandment: first love of God, second love of neighbor as one loves self (Mark 12:31).[32]

Clearly, FAPC echoes other black Presbyterians who believe that before a congregation can become an instrument of God in the world it must harness its love of God and self in ways that find expression in community. It is from this perspective that the leadership of FAPC chose to emerge from its "valley experiences" of the late 1990s and adopt a serious back-to-basics effort for the new millenium. Focusing on the need to love God and self, they recommitted to a focus on basic Christian doctrine, the reorganization and retooling of leadership, and a serious reflection on stewardship of time, talents, and treasures. In each case their study, training, and reflection centered on what it meant to love God and love self.

Out of this reorientation emerged a more explicit emphasis on Cooperative Economics that really had its genesis as early as 1994. During those early years, said Lomax, "The deacon board and the Eropo Men's Ministry led the way in the partnership with Habitat for Humanity and the Atlantans Building Leadership for Empowerment (ABLE). For three to four years, they organized First Afrikan members to help build a house a year in conjunction with other congregations in DeKalb County." In 2001 they revisited that vision and began to seriously discuss ways to further develop it in the new millenium. This resulted in more explicit efforts toward Cooperative Economics in the form of the First Afrikan Community Development Corporation (FACDC). The threefold mission of this 501(c)3 organization seeks to:

1. Establish a partnership with the community for the purpose of revitalization and development,

2. Conduct a needs assessment and market analysis of the city of Lithonia, Georgia, and surrounding communities, and

3. Develop a community center that will include programs to address the economic, housing, family and recreational needs of the community.

Deborah Jackson was one of the key members of this planning team for the new development corporation.[33] As a member of FAPC since 2000, this attorney helped to secure the incorporation papers and complete the 501(c)3 application. Her legal background in addition to experience in financial planning and real estate prepared her for the task ahead, which would require an assessment of the legal, economic, and property realities of the Lithonia community. This small town has approximately twenty-two hundred people, is 80 percent African American, and has an African American mayor. Jackson observed that the city "has a high level of poverty but is surrounded by wealth." Although the church is located in unincorporated Lithonia she believes that its commitment should move toward revitalizing this town.

Officially, the Atlanta Regional Commission deals with the planning of the various municipalities. The vision of FACDC, however, as articulated by Jackson, is that "We have an opportunity as well as a responsibility to develop mechanisms to make sure that our needs and the concerns as a community are no longer overlooked."[34] Even more specifically, she continued, "FAPC has the opportunity to play a very unique role in terms of filling the gap from a much more holistic perspective." A part of the initial vision for implementation is to conduct a feasibility study to assess the need and then provide information/educational seminars and workshops to raise the consciousness of the community, to encourage commitment to their overall plan, and to prepare the families for the change. The overall vision of the FACDC is to cultivate in southeast DeKalb County, "a world-respected, self-sustaining, economically sound, academically excellent, faith-based community that serves as a model for all people."[35]

The early stages of the plan, seen through the lens of Cooperative Economics, frames the work of education, spiritual formation/Bible study, and pastoral care as dimensions of Cooperative Economics that seek to develop and nurture the existing material, intellectual, spiritual, and human capital of the congregation. With this as a backdrop, the further development of FACDC will become more than an isolated effort within the community. It will, through faith, begin to build bridges and fill gaps that holistically and Africentrically link the congregation with the community. Three important entities of FAPC ministry will lead the way; they are the Kilombo Pan African Institute, the Black Kabbalah Institute and the Uhuru Community Caregivers.

Aminata Umoja, a key member on the planning committee of the Kilombo Pan African Institute (KPAI) affirms the institute's vision and mission for a holistic teaching/learning experience.[36] This woman, who describes herself as a "revolutionary nationalist" and was active for many years in the New African Independent Movement, joined FAPC with a mind to use her gifts and insights as an educator to imagine and develop an innovative education program for children and youth. Through the leadership of Umoja and others, the KPAI envisions a comprehensive after-school program that will later grow into education for elementary school and beyond. The curriculum will be built upon Maatian principles that view education as a task that is at once physical, spiritual, intellectual, and relational. "KPAI will not be a *Christian* school," she said, "but a *spiritual* school that welcomes all faiths. Africanness," she continued, "will not be an add-on but the basic framework for all curriculum." Fueled by a strong sense of Self-Determination, the KPAI is also an expression of Cooperative Economics as it intentionally plans to tap into, develop, and use intellectual capital through education and study and spiritual capital through faith formation and character building. In the long run, as imagined in the opening vignette, it has the potential for expressions beyond elementary school as it prepares a new generation of women and men, "to think critically, work collectively, live communally and transform entirely the Afrikan and world communities."[37]

In a similar way, Gene Stephenson found a way to further develop his commitment to Cooperative Economics through the development of intellectual and spiritual capital in the Black Kabbalah Institute (BKI). This former Black Panther and member of the Nation of Islam said that he was, "energized by the fact that FAPC was a teaching church."[38] As one of the students in the BKI, which approaches adult Bible study from a perspective that embraces both west and east Afrikan spiritualities, he affirms that "critical Bible study helps eliminate an enslaved mentality." Drawing from the Kabbalah tradition that arose within Judaism as mystical teachings and practices that promoted inner wisdom about self and God, this institute "seeks to teach and apply the Kabbalah as an interpretive resource for the enrichment of Afrikan/American spiritual and psychological health."[39]

In the spirit of education for transformation in the world, advanced study in the Bible through the BKI encourages a critical reading of the text that acknowledges the broad, "geographical, social, cultural, economic, and political world view that existed throughout that part of the ancient world."[40] A more critical study of the Bible, said Coleman, awakens one "from the deep sleep of biblical literalism and acquires a [more profound] appreciation of how to read and comprehend its text and stories." He believes that the goal should not be to simply "believe in the Bible" but to come to know God in a way that gives a "deeper understanding of who and what you are, especially as an African American created and creating in God's image." Through the lens of Cooperative Economics the BKI views this level of learning as an essential part of congregational stewardship of intellectual and spiritual capital that leads to transformation of individuals and communities and not simply a commitment to knowledge for the sake of knowledge.

In addition to the cultivation of intellectual and spiritual capital, the FACDC is also committed to the gifts and promises of emotional and psychological health as a way to develop human resources. Dr. Teresa Snorton, for example, said she joined FAPC, "because it nurtured and challenged me on both a spiritual and intellectual level."[41] But this former pastor and current chaplain and Certified Supervisor of Clinical Pastoral Education also came to FAPC with a deep concern about the health and wholeness of families and communities. The Uhuru Community Care-givers (UCC) with its focus on "pastoral care, counseling, crisis interven-tion, relationship-building skills, spiritual enrichment, education, and consultation for individuals and families and congregations who are seek-ing healing and wholeness," became the ideal place for her to work. Dr. Snorton affirms the congregational commitment to meet "the multifac-eted needs of an emerging African American middle class."[42] She goes on to say that "the healing and wholeness needed for this constituency are connected to the adoption of African-centered values that stress cooper-ation rather than competition, [hence] the middle-class tendency to strive for individualism must be replaced with communalism." In the spirit of Cooperative Economics, Snorton and the UCC focus on the meaning of Uhuru—freedom—as an opportunity to experience communal sharing linked to responsibility rather than individual self-service fueled by com-petition. This strengthens the human resources of the community.

It is important to note that this notion of healing and wholeness through communal sharing and responsibility are not restricted to con-gregational life. Through the lens of Cooperative Economics, the culti-vation and maintenance of emotional, psychological, and spiritual cap-ital is the goal for the community at large. It will require collaboration, cooperation, and consultation among religious institutions and social service and health agencies alike, creating a web of support that moves individuals and families beyond simply surviving to thriving. Through leaders like Dr. Snorton, the UCC will be instrumental in restoring wholeness and preparing the church and community for meaningful and transforming contributions in the world.

The resiliency and complexities of congregational life are seen quite clearly in the story of FAPC. Through the lenses of Self-Determination and Cooperative Economics we see an example of a "thick" congregational identity as characterized by Hopewell that has multiple layers of meaning. In its story, FAPC uncovers the value of viewing, at once, its past and present identity in anticipation of who it will be in the future. In the process this congregation has risen as a phoenix out of the smoldering ashes of Salem Presbyterian Church to become a community of faith committed to Self-Determination and Cooperative Economics. In the work of ministry, these two principles act as a set of bifocal lenses. Self-Determination allows the members to see the fine print of their identity and to appreciate the intricacies and details of their culture. Cooperative Economics gives them a vision beyond themselves with a much broader peripheral view that spans the horizon and detects other perspectives. Either of these lenses alone would produce a ministry focus that is inappropriate and ineffective for the needs of the African American community today. But when used together they yield a strong and realistic view of the challenges and promise for that community for today and beyond. Through its ministry and mission, FAPC is learning the appropriate use of its bifocal lenses as it continues to truly walk the talk and keep the faith.

WALKIN' THE TALK OF SELF-DETERMINATION AND COOPERATIVE ECONOMICS

Self-Determination

This principle on the surface brings to mind thoughts of self-actualization through rugged individualism. This is not a foreign concept in America where a "bootstrap ideology" has historically been lauded and encouraged. Viewed for nearly four hundred years as the land of opportunity, this country has attracted great numbers of immigrants who have successfully moved up the ladder of success by sheer will and tenacity. But the other side of the story is that in this same land of opportunity there have also been great numbers of people who were unable to progress. Some suggest that this failure to achieve is simply a matter of not trying hard enough but others know, from experience, that all the determination in the world is useless if there are obstacles built in that prevent forward movement.

African Americans are among some in this country that have been systematically prevented from progress. One of the historic reasons for this is that their entrance into this country was under duress; therefore, the world they encountered was not of their own making or choosing. They also entered a society that had an unapologetic disdain for their African lineage that translated into a disregard of their very humanity. In each case, the establishment of a healthy self-understanding was essential for them to survive as well as thrive and required a strong sense of Self-Determination.

Karenga says that an important step toward Self-Determination for persons of African descent in America is to recognize both the "right and responsibility to exist as a people and to make our own unique contribution to the forward flow of human history."[43] This statement is a response to nearly four centuries of diminished rights and disregarded contributions. The net result has created a deficit for all—those of African descent as well as those who are not—because it fails to appreciate and learn from the "forward flow of human history" as a whole in America. In this same sense, seeking Self-Determination is a conscious goal for the members of FAPC. Through their name alone, they boldly declare their connection to an ancestral past and through their ministries they embrace the right and responsibility to name and claim their reality and destiny. This declaration finds even deeper meaning when one considers the physical location of this congregation: Atlanta, Georgia, the heart of the Jim/"Jane" Crow South. But despite this regional reality, a spirit of Self-Determination prevailed in the African American community through efforts toward celebrating heritage, claiming the right to exist and seeking to not only survive but to thrive.

A look at the redefined principle, however, gives yet another dimension of Self-Determination when seen through the lens of Faith: *"To define ourselves as daughters and sons of Africa, created in the image of God and willing to participate in the liberation of those in the Diaspora and the world."* While this restated definition is very close to Karenga's that speaks of the importance *"to define ourselves, name ourselves, create for ourselves and speak for ourselves,"* the difference comes in the locus of these self-determining actions. The new definition attempts to balance culture and faith in the crucible of a communal reality grounded in God, not simply in human effort as suggested in the old definition. This small but critical variance is essential for the life and ministry of FAPC precisely because of the added reality of what it means to be a part of the African Diaspora that is located in the deep South of America. This racial/historical legacy alone suggests the need for a level of Self-Determination at FAPC that is grounded first and foremost in a liberating spirit of God that neutralizes and diminishes fear and helplessness as well as self-hatred and communal fragmentation.

The restated definition is more intentional about defining, naming, creating, and speaking in the context of relationship with Africa and with God. Africa is mentioned first in this definition not because it is the more important of the two but because it represents the undeniable reality of culture. Claiming relationship with Africa as daughters and sons implies a familial connection that links this congregation to the historical as well as ancestral past. Acknowledging solidarity to others in their struggle for liberation is an important extension of this identity. It is therefore necessary and fitting to celebrate the continuing presence and impact of those who are connected with them through ancestry as well as those who are now only present in the spirit. Being self-determined in this instance depends on an abiding notion of communality that transcends time and space.

Their emphasis on an Afrikan/Black Messiah is a clear expression of this Africa/God connection. An Afrikan/Black Messiah acknowledges the ethnic/geographic proximity of Jesus to the continent of Africa and aligns very closely to that of Albert Cleage as discussed in *The Black Christ* by Kelly Brown Douglas. She points out that his emphasis on the ethnicity of Jesus was based on his genealogical relationship to black Americans as a black man.[44] It was an effort to "make the Christian gospel relevant to a Black people who rarely experienced relief from psychological and physical burden in White racism."[45] It also sought to free the black church of the 1960s from the captivity of "slaveholding Christianity" and to marry black nationalism and Christianity in the model of Marcus Garvey.[46] While FAPC does not display the same kind of explicit commitment to black Christian nationalism through separation as did many in that earlier era, it is aware of the value of focusing on an Afrikan/Black Messiah who looks like African people and responds to their concerns in the contemporary context. This translates into a need to liberate Jesus in the contemporary context from the historical bonds of whiteness and encourages this act of liberation to continue in the hearts, minds, and ministry of this congregation through Self-Determination.

But to anchor the primary source of Self-Determination in the human experience of being African in the Diaspora alone is to run the risk of worshiping blackness and deifying the ancestors. The second part of this definition, therefore, places the more concrete reality of culture into its proper perspective in the divine cosmos. It grounds primary identity in the image of God in both the divinity and the humanity of an Afrikan/Black Christ, which becomes the source of individual and communal identities. To be created in the image of God then is to ground one's identity in a divine locus while continuing to honor cultural particularities. Beginning with a belief in the goodness of God's creation provides a platform upon which the members of FAPC can affirm the fullness of both individual and communal identities that find their source in a God who affirms and loves their culture.

When we look at this congregation's focus on ancestors and affirmation of an Afrikan/Black Messiah in their prayers and rituals, we see evidence of such a transfer. Some may interpret the focus on ancestors as un-Christian and the emphasis of an Afrikan/Black Messiah as a gesture of separatism when, for FAPC, they are a marriage between an aspect of an African cosmology and a Christian theology. It is this level of integration between faith and culture that sustains this congregation's developing notion of Self-Determination through their strong belief in one's ability to name reality and destiny, and it is supported by the mystery and meaning found in the divine power and presence that sustains the cosmos.

Cooperative Economics

This principle, as with Self-Determination, essentially speaks for itself as it affirms the collaborative and mutually responsible use of resources for the good of the community. The resources that initially come to mind are material in nature as they relate to employment, housing, and business. Karenga's description of Cooperative Economics that seek to "build and maintain our own stores, shops and other businesses and to profit from them together," provides a very attractive solution for African Americans in this city. It encourages them to capitalize on the promise and to solve some of the problems faced by Atlanta's economic reality. This understanding of Cooperative Economics has historic examples in the efforts made by African Americans during the late nineteenth and early twentieth centuries when the black community needed to find ways to move from surviving to thriving. Booker T. Washington was a prominent leader during this time who advocated self-help, racial solidarity, and accommodation as a solution. He found his greatest opponent, however, in W. E. B. Du Bois. This scholar countered with a platform of political action, civil rights, and the need to develop an educated elite—"the Talented Tenth"—from within the African American community, who would be major spokespersons on behalf of the black masses.

The classic Washington/Du Bois debate reveals two different ways to improve life for African Americans. It is, however, Washington's version that aligns more closely with Karenga's understanding of Cooperative Economics. In each case, the focus is on self-help and racial solidarity through economic empowerment from within rather than political action with and among those outside of the black community. But a look at the renewed description of this principle gives a more appropriate and empowering interpretation in a congregational context. In this definition, Cooperative Economics is *to believe in and demonstrate a holistic, multidimensional stewardship that values all our resources, including material, human, intellectual, and spiritual resources as gifts from God to be developed and used in African American communities, the Diaspora, and the world for the good of all people.*

When Cooperative Economics is viewed in terms of hard resources and profits, there is the tendency to place the ultimate worth in the bricks and mortar or in bank statements and spreadsheets. While focusing on building, maintaining, and profiting is one of the outcomes that FAPC seeks, there is a desire to place more emphasis on the nature and source of the resources themselves. Material resources, then, are seen on the same par with human, intellectual, and spiritual capital and it is in the cultivation and development of these latter three that the more obvious material resources are kept in proper perspective. One of the goals of the FACDC, for example, is providing affordable housing. Rather than simply identifying sites and constructing structures, this plan also includes workshops, seminars, and classes to prepare the community for the responsibilities of a renewed environment. This recognizes the presence and capacity for developing *intellectual capital* within the community as people are challenged to think critically about and respond to their situations. In a similar way, providing pastoral counseling for the community is seen as more than a way to help persons address the crises of the moment. It is an attempt at moving toward a deeper spiritual awareness and therefore a more holistic healing that leads to the acceptance of both personal and communal responsibilities. This acknowledges the opportunity to cultivate *spiritual capital* that provides a way to reestablish through ongoing faith formation lives that have been fragmented, while pointing toward hope for the future. Each of these examples, in turn, will cultivate *human capital* in the community as individuals and families take ownership of their present lives and begin to envision new possibilities for tomorrow. Viewing material, human, intellectual, and spiritual resources as gifts from God shifts the perception of obligation from profits for the community to good stewardship for God. When this obligation is centered on one's community alone, it runs the risk of selective distribution and opens the way for exploitation as the rich get richer and the poor remain poor. When the obligation is centered on the Divine, however, it is empowered by a different source. There is a celebration and cultivation of gifts beyond the material, creating a more holistic notion of Cooperative Economics, shifting the emphasis from profit to stewardship.

This understanding of communal resources as multidimensional and holistically linked to divine stewardship reflects five functional dynamics of African American spiritual praxis described by Carlyle F. Stewart. He describes them as "*formation* of black consciousness, black communitas, and black culture; the *unification* of self and community; and the *corroboration* of values, meaning and existence for African American people and the *transformation* and *consecration* of black life as a sacred reality."[47] Of the five components, I believe that transformation and consecration of black life as a sacred reality aligns most closely to the development and use of human, intellectual, spiritual, and material capital through Cooperative Economics. It begins with the assets of black existence and is sensitive to the need for a proactive trajectory that supports an active expression of freedom.[48] This expression of freedom is not restricted to the building of institutions but is seen as the springboard for transformation in the larger culture and society. Thus Cooperative Economics, viewed through the lens of faith, broadens its scope and deepens its commitment in ways that illustrate the spiritual sense of stewardship so essential in an Africentric congregational context.

four

Trinity United Church of Christ

Unity and Purpose

THE CONGREGATIONAL STORY

One afternoon in June 1976 Romney Payne rose to give the valedictorian speech at her eighth-grade graduation. In this year of America's bicentennial this was, however, not the typical graduation address of congratulations and patriotism. This speech advocated a global connection between youth across the world to courageously address the political, economic, and social crises of the day. At the heart of her protest was her awakening to the level of oppression in the world, the silence of most secular and religious leaders, and their inability to move toward substantive change. As a high school student, she left her home church and joined the Young Socialist League, where she found a platform for her passion and commitment in the anti-apartheid movement.

Although ostracized by family, friends, and teachers because of her views, she said, "As a young person, I was trying to understand why the church was not a part of the solution. It became clear to me," she continued, "that it wasn't simply a matter of politics but it was also a spiritual issue."[1] She consequently questioned the inability of the Socialist Party to see the value of including a spiritual dimension to their work. At the same time she still could not reconcile the reluctance of the church to take the lead as an agent of change through more organized efforts.[2] What she sought was a sense of unity that could bring together the best of the church and political organizations, as they rallied around a common purpose that combined doctrine and ideology with justice.

It was later, in 1982, as she traveled to an anti-apartheid rally that her search took a surprising twist. On the lawn of a small church she saw a sign that read "Free South Africa," and the following Sunday she attended that church out of sheer curiosity. The service was well attended, the music was inspiring, and the sermon linked, very clearly, the mandate of the gospel with the social and political issues of the day. "The first sermon," she recalled, "was about apartheid and other things going on in the world. I heard a clear connectedness between people here and people in Africa and I said 'yes!' in my spirit." While its content was not remotely connected to the socialist rhetoric of her affiliated organization, this sermon's emphasis on the evil of apartheid and the responsibility of the church in eradicating this system was music to her ears. She heard a subtle but definite commitment to unity with African people across the globe and acknowledgment of a purpose that found its locus in the God of liberation and justice. Soon after, she joined that community of faith, Trinity United Church of Christ, in Chicago, Illinois, where she became active in a number of ministries, one being the United Black Christians (UBC).[3]

The UBC was a caucus of black laity, clergy, and youth across the country that sought to maximize the responsiveness of the United Church of Christ (UCC) to the needs of the black community.[4] In addition to encouraging a sense of unity among African Americans in the larger denominational network, the UBC also developed a number of strong local leaders who believed that their main purpose was to call to task the denomination's espoused commitment to justice and equality. In 1977 the Chicago Chapter of the UBC was founded and its first chairperson, S. L. Allen, took a major leadership role. "Before Mr. Allen's tenure," said Patricia Eggleston, one of the early members, "the UBC had limited voice, exposure, and impact in the larger denomination. Under his leadership, however, they gained financial autonomy, developed new leadership, and created stronger bonds of accountability between black clergy and the denomination."[5]

It is important to note, however, that this zeal toward activism displayed by Allen was not always his response. Having joined Trinity in 1966, he admits to being less than enthusiastic about church work early on. "In the early days," he recalled, "I attended church on Sunday but I was just not active." It was, however, in 1972 after a small gathering at the home of the newly installed pastor, Rev. Jeremiah A. Wright Jr., that he decided to assume a more active posture. "When I went to the meeting, he sounded like he would be okay so I decided to give the brother a break," he said. So Allen stepped away from the sidelines and into the full life of the congregation. First as a trustee and later as the chair of the Executive Council, his sense of personal commitment began to evolve. Soon he became a very bold and vocal presence in the life of the local church and the denomination as he asked hard questions. He pushed the envelope as he challenged them to walk the talk and live out the purpose that they professed.[6]

These are only two of the many individual stories that are a part of the history of Trinity United Church of Christ, a congregation that has become known across the nation as being "Unashamedly Black and Unapologetically Christian." It would be a mistake, however, to conclude that the vision and commitment toward Unity and Purpose that was displayed by Trinity in the 1980s came forth fully grown in the life of this congregation. A closer look at its early story will reveal a very difficult journey that led them to this place as well as very small but significant seeds of Unity and Purpose that were germinating in the hearts and minds of Trinity members from its inception.

Trinity United Church of Christ marks its natal day as December 3, 1961, when twelve families gathered in the gymnasium of a local elementary school in Chicago for their first worship service. Many of its members had been a part of the southward migration within the city as African Americans, moving into the middle-class stratum of urban society, began to push beyond the boundaries of the "Black Belt"[7] of the city's South Side. This migration was a part of a larger one that was evident across the nation as middle-class whites moved to the suburbs during the 1950s and 1960s.[8] This move away from urban centers left homes vacant that were gradually filled by upwardly mobile African Americans. Likewise, as church buildings grew in the white suburbs, many edifices left empty in the city were purchased and filled by middle-class black congregants. Part of the excitement of this body gathered on that December morning resulted from the fact that they would not occupy a vacated white church. They would soon build their own!

"As a new church, started by the Chicago Congregational Christian Association of the UCC," recalled Kenneth B. Smith, the founding pastor, "Trinity was originally envisioned as an integrated church that would have black and white copastors."[9] This was a particularly bold plan in light of the historic patterns of segregated housing in Chicago. In this part of the city, Halsted Street marked the color line, with white families to the west and black families to the east. S. L. and Barbara Allen, however, were among the black families that transgressed the barrier and settled on the West Side. "There were burnings of black homes in our neighborhood," said S. L. Allen. "A group of whites even decided one day to have a picnic on one of my neighbor's lawns." These and other racial realities made talk of a merger between a new black congregation and a white church in the nearby suburb unfeasible. Instead, the Association made a conscious effort to start a new church for this rapidly growing black middle-class community in Chicago's far southern corridor east of Halsted Street.

What becomes obvious in this turn of events is that the Association had a specific agenda in mind—the inclusion of a certain kind of black church. Only four blocks east of Trinity's permanent site and twenty years before its founding sat a federally funded housing community. This community, along with other public housing complexes throughout the city, was not a target for new church starts of the Congregational Christian Church or the UCC—they did not include the right kind of black people. Hence, the major impetus behind the founding of Trinity Church by the Association was the spread of the Christian gospel, guided by an obvious class preference toward the African American members of this new community. "Historically," explained Rev. Dr. W. Sterling Cary, the first African American conference minister in the UCC, "the Association made special efforts to seek out 'high potential'

churches within the black community. These were," he continued, ·
"African American congregations and communities that were more
likely to assimilate into the form and function of the denomination."[10]
It was, therefore, this racial reality that informed the planting of Trinity
UCC on the South Side of Chicago.

In 1961 the Association called the Rev. Kenneth B. Smith, who had
served for the past four years as lay associate minister at the Congregational
Church of Park Manor in Chicago. A former Catholic from Montclair,
New Jersey, Smith said, "I became disenchanted with my childhood faith
while at Fisk University but later found inspiration and mentorship in the
person of William J. Faulkner, the dean."[11] He joined with twelve families
from four black South Side congregations, accepted the challenge issued
by the Association to blaze the Congregational trail further south, and
helped found Trinity United Church of Christ.[12] The first five years of
Trinity's history saw steady growth. "One of the many challenges that we
faced as we attempted to garner support and members for our new church
was to explain the obscurity of the name United Church of Christ," said
Smith. Still in its infancy (only formed in 1957), this new denomination
was, "virtually unknown and too often confused with the Church of
Christ or the Church of God in Christ by prospective members," he
added. Although Trinity was technically the first new African American
church in Chicago to wear the name UCC, they chose to use the
Congregational title, adding it in parenthesis to their official name, to distinguish them from their white fundamentalist and independent black denominational counterparts. Most of these members were first generation
Congregationalists coming from earlier Baptist and Methodist congregations, and they had no real idea of the richness and depth of the
Congregational heritage with its strong Puritan lineage. Their mere association with a white denomination, however, gave them a sense of both
Unity and Purpose within the mainline religious tradition of America.[13]

In their comfortable existence as a new and growing community of
faith, Trinity's main purpose was to be a fellowship of Christians who
followed the style of worship and polity of the UCC and to make
available the traditional church ministries and programs. In addition to
their works of ministry, they also exhibited an emerging spirit of activism, mirroring and affirming the larger denominational commitment
to justice and equality.

The march from Montgomery to Selma in 1965 organized by Dr. Martin Luther King Jr. and the Southern Christian Leadership Conference (SCLC), for example, excited their civic concern for the issue of voter discrimination in the South. "To show our solidarity with the cause," said Smith, "the congregation supported my trip to Alabama to be a part of this historic five-day march. In my absence, they made picket signs and joined a group of Chicagoans who staged a local march in support of the cause." Here their efforts to halt discriminatory practices toward their sisters and brothers in the South stood in stark contrast to their obvious blind spot of the Association's position on church growth among African Americans in Chicago—one that supported only middle-class churches. In this state of myopia, unfortunately, the young Trinity was unable to challenge the class discrimination exhibited by the denomination as vigorously as they did the issue of voter discrimination by southern leaders.

The climax of this early history was the move into their first modest but efficient facility in 1966. The new site was chosen for its convenient location and its agreeable price. But even more revealing was the apparent reluctance by the Association to venture west of the racial line drawn in the city that restricted the settling of African Americans.[14] The new church, which seated up to two hundred, was located, therefore, close enough to a main thoroughfare to provide ready transportation yet comfortably nestled among ranch-style, Georgian, and split level homes in a young and growing African American community.

The church was designed with the help of a black firm, the Robert Martin Construction Company. "There was intentional visual reference to the theological significance of the name Trinity," said Smith, "using triangular forms in the stained glass windows." While their efforts were financially supervised and supported for the first five years by the Church Extension Committee of the Chicago Congregational Association, this young congregation engaged in numerous fund-raisers to reduce their debt. This prevented them from becoming what they called an "ADC church (aid for dependent churches)," said Smith, exhibiting a strong sense of independence. The first five years culminated with this historic move from the gymnasium of a local elementary school to a new building and saw growth, prosperity, and a continuing sense of Unity around black middle-class life and values and membership in the UCC. The five that followed, however, began with an event that forged the first deep crack in their secure, middle-class Congregational foundation: the resignation of their founding pastor[15] and a significant decline in membership.

The second pastor of Trinity was the Rev. Willie J. Jamerson.[16] He arrived at Trinity in the fall of 1966 by way of Roanoke, Virginia, at the height of the civil rights movement. Jamerson recalled that after his experiences of protest and arrest, "I brought a desire to comfort the afflicted and afflict the comfortable and I was convinced that the church was the place where this could best be done." In retrospect, he added, "I was perhaps drawn more to the role of prophet than that of priest." This kind of vision, in light of the day-to-day demands of a young congregation just moving into a new facility, placed a tremendous damper on his goal of activism. "Many members of the congregation," he continued, "needed to be comforted more than challenged and the major purpose of the church was to affirm their middle-class Congregationalism." This further constricted his vision and placed additional strain on the ministry, resulting in continued decline in membership.

In the middle of this transitional period between 1966 and 1971, the members of Trinity were adjusting to the change in leadership and a dwindling membership in their local arena. On the national front, however, the African American community experienced the loss of their own prophetic leader in the assassination of Dr. Martin Luther King Jr. in 1968, forging a second crack in Trinity's middle-class, Congregational foundation. Immediately followed by fires and violence, this tragic event later spiraled into a time of pensive silence and mournful reflection across the nation concerning the *real* feasibility of racial unity in America.[17] The failure of the civil rights movement to usher in an era of genuine integration and harmony between the races turned into a search for an alternative experience of purpose and belonging for many African Americans.

The Black Power movement filled the void left by the civil rights movement for many and encouraged them to validate their own experiences—even their religious experiences. Consequently, white denominations across the country saw an exodus of some of their black members who sought churches that honored their religious and cultural heritages—churches that sought to combine black identity and Christian commitment.[18] Trinity Church and the other black churches across the nation, however, trusted in the promises of America to honor and affirm their achievements as citizens regardless of their color. They saw no significance in highlighting the fact of race and chose instead to strive for Unity around the larger category of being part of the Christian Church.

While Trinity, as a community of faith, did not place a high priority on the black consciousness movement at this time, there were a few members within the body who did. During "Negro History Week" in the late 1960s, when the children in the fourth grade church school class were asked by their teachers to report on important living figures within the black community, "One young man reported on Malcolm X, to our delight," said Barbara Allen, one of the teachers. "But when news of this report got out, an emergency meeting of the church school staff was called following a parent's complaint."[19] This parent, speaking on behalf of most families of the church, strongly believed that the purpose of the church school was to teach children Jesus and this was an inappropriate setting for "Negro" history lessons. "The other teachers and I made it a regular habit to color faces brown on all church school materials, because we saw no separation between our black identity and their Christian commitment," Allen added. But in light of the heavy opposition and in a spirit of dismay, she withdrew from regular worship, only devoting time to the children in church school.

This experience of disappointment on the local level for these teachers and a few others at Trinity was compounded by the general state of racial unrest in the nation, creating a real crisis of identity between their blackness and their Christianity. The majority of this congregation, however, held tenaciously to their Congregational tradition, finding Unity in their connection to American Protestantism and Purpose in the lifestyle of black "middle-classness."[20] They had no thought of embracing a black religious tradition grounded in an emerging black theology but were instead invested in what Vallmer E. Jordan described as the "pursuit of social status and the trappings of upward mobility."[21] These members were stuck in a kind of time warp that shielded them from the transforming effects of the turbulent 1960s. In 1967, for example, Rev. Jamerson received a call from the Black Panther Party asking if the church could be one of the sites of their Breakfast Program.[22] "I did not even pass that information to my

Council," he recalled, "because I knew it would not fly." This was in light of earlier unsuccessful efforts to involve the church in Operation Breadbasket.[23] Ironically, by 1971 when their peak of 250 members had dwindled down under one hundred, they could not quite figure what had gone wrong. By this time, Jamerson decided to move on to another position and Trinity was faced with the dilemma of searching for a third pastor or simply closing the doors.

One of the first indications of a shift in their sense of Purpose became apparent in December 1971. Now, under the leadership of an interim pastor, Reuben A. Sheares III,[24] the remaining leaders began to grapple with what was *really* going on at Trinity. "For years we had prided ourselves on being a middle-class congregation within a mainline denomination, but suddenly the values within the black community had shifted," said Jordan. "Aspirations for integration and assimilation were being replaced by those of black pride and separation." This new reality was a difficult one for Trinity to fathom because it threatened the secure sense of racial unity they felt and depended on as black members of a white denomination. It was no longer enough to simply carry a picket sign in support of a noble black cause, confident that a nonviolent approach would gently convict the dominant culture of its inequities. It was now time to be proactive about social reform—to be intentionally involved in making meaningful changes from inside the black community. It was now time to rethink the present purpose, philosophy, and position of this dying congregation and create a new direction that would envision the kind of church they needed to be— essentially the kind of church they had failed to be.

This quest resulted in the drafting of a congregational "job description" for the church by Jordan, who served as the chair of the Pulpit Committee. It was an enhanced mission statement that laid the groundwork and re-defined the direction for the next phase of Trinity's growth as they sought among other things to be:

> a source of spiritual sustenance, security, and inspiration; that those participating in our spiritual-social process [may] be strengthened in their commitment . . . to serve as instruments of God and church in our communities and the world, confronting, transforming and eliminating those things in our cul-

ture that lead to the dehumanization of persons and tend to perpetuate their psychological enslavement.[25]

"We gave this document to each of the prospective candidates[26] recommended by the Association," said Jordan, "asking them if they could lead us in this direction." It was, however, the interview on December 31, 1971, of Rev. Jeremiah A. Wright Jr., he recalled, that ended the search. "His educational credentials were impressive in themselves." He was a graduate of Howard University with a Bachelor of Arts in English and a Master of Arts in The History of Religions from the University of Chicago, where he was currently a doctoral student. He had also served as associate minister at Beth Eden Baptist Church in Chicago. "But it was his excitement and vision for the task at hand," said Jordan, "that came through most pointedly as he answered another one of the key questions of each interview, 'How do you see the role of the Black Church in the black struggle?'" Jordan recalled that Wright's response singled him out as the only possible leader for Trinity Church; thus he was voted in by the Congregation the second Sunday in February, 1972, as their new pastor.

Despite this exciting congregational job description, the full support of the Pulpit Committee, and the vote of the congregation, this newly called pastor, a native of Philadelphia, from a line of preachers including his mother and father, still faced a formidable challenge. It should be noted that, in the congregational job description, the committee made no direct references to being black. "We saw no need to use this term because we believed that our ethnic identity was understood and we were afraid that [such references] might be offensive to those outside of the African American community," said Jordan. Moreover, while Wright anticipated an agenda of black pride and affirmation, many Trinitarians still found comfort and esteem in their ability to assimilate. "One of the earliest questions I candidly asked the congregation," said Wright, "was whether they wanted to be a white church in black face or a black church in the black community?"

In the midst of the black consciousness revolution that swept the nation, Trinity was confronted with the reality of its own "double consciousness."[27] The staunch adherence to the Eurocentric religious tradition of Congregationalism that this community of faith emulated began to lose its comfortable fit in the environment of black consciousness and revolution. Even their earlier support of the civil rights movement was challenged, as the African Americans of the nation lost faith in American systems and sought empowerment through self-help and revolution. It was at this point in its journey as a small and struggling congregation— small in its numbers as well as its vision and struggling for its survival as well as its identity—that Trinity decided to begin the painful process of shedding the shame associated with blackness and claiming a new Purpose that called them to a Christianity of liberation and empowerment.

So at what point did Trinity UCC move away from its narrow self-understanding and move on to embrace the Unity and Purpose illustrated in the mid-1970s and early 1980s? There are a number vignettes from this congregational story that illustrate that shift; however, a major turning point took place on the fifth Sunday of October 1972 as the members of Trinity gathered for morning worship. This Sunday marked a departure from the familiar routine because it was the beginning of a long tradition of Youth Sundays, instituted by Wright. It was an opportunity for the young people to be responsibile for leading worship, from the processional to the benediction. This was inspired by a request from the youth to their new pastor to start a youth choir only three months after his installation. "I told them to meet with the minister of music and rehearse a few times and then call me so that I could come and hear them when they were ready," he recalled. After several weeks of rehearsal, however, they complained that the director could not play gospel music, which they really wanted to sing. This led to a request by the youth to the Executive Council to hire a promising musician who grew up with them. His name was Jeffrey P. Radford.[28] Under the leadership of the new director, the Youth Fellowship Choir processed on the Youth Sunday in October in red and green dashikis over black turtle neck tops and black pants or skirts, rather than the traditional choir robes, singing gospel music. Through both visual and musical presentation, this young choir ushered in a new day at Trinity Church, and through their music they ignited the flame that would burn off the dross of black shame to reveal the refined gem of self-love.

Not all in the congregation welcomed this new day. A spirit of uneasiness and discontent about the inevitable change had already become apparent at Wright's first congregational meeting in July 1972 in the form of protest over a change in hymnals. Later opposition over the purchase of an organ and even near mutiny within the Chancel Choir resulted over the shift to gospel music. "In totality," said Wright, "these crises amounted to the fear of change—change in the style of worship but, more importantly, change in the kind of members that would desire to join our church." Even so, the wheels were in motion for a major shift in Trinity's sense of both Unity and Purpose.

The next ten to fifteen years was a time of numerical as well as spiritual and cultural growth for Trinity. From the humble number of eighty-seven in 1972, the membership grew steadily to over four thousand by 1987. Likewise, through Wright's early leadership, the members began to slowly move away from the concept of church as a place to enhance and validate their social position to one that appreciated church as a place for spiritual formation. Although the bulletins, newsletters, and other documents produced during that time still noted much energy devoted toward social activities, they also revealed a growing sense of God-consciousness. The May 1972 Board of Deacons newsletter, for example, encouraged members to take heed of the following worship attitude posted in the bulletin each Sunday by Wright:

> The Prelude is a veil draped between life and the sanctuary. The music, when you cross the threshold, should separate the world without from the world within. If you must whisper, let it be a prayer.

This new discipline realigned the old purpose of Sunday worship that stressed the social, intellectual, and moral dimensions of the congregation's life to also include, more explicitly, the spiritual. This move toward a more spirit-centered focus found other small yet illustrative examples in the areas of prayer and ministry devotions. Regardless of the reason for a gathering or the number of persons present, for example, opening devotion and closing prayer became a permanent part of every meeting agenda. As awkward as it felt at the beginning, members began to establish a sense of God-consciousness that became the foundation upon which all church business was built, focusing less on fellowship and more on ministry.

In addition to the renewed discipline of prayer and devotion, worship became more vibrant through music. As the ministry of music grew, it included multiple choirs moving beyond the traditional hymns, anthems, and arranged Negro spirituals that they were accustomed to singing. Pastor Wright and Mr. Radford added contemporary gospel music, traditional gospel music, meter singing, and African music! In 1973, the Youth

Fellowship Choir's name was changed to the Trinity Choral Ensemble (TCE) so that adults could join the choir, and that choir soon outstripped the Chancel Choir. "In 1977," said Wright, "the two choirs were combined to form the Sanctuary Choir of the Trinity United Church of Christ. From that point we would no longer have two congregations, with one set of members coming on Sundays that the Chancel Choir sang and the other set of members coming when the TCE sang."

In addition to the musical innovations, the call and response mode of black worship increased as members became more comfortable hearing shouts of "Amen" during sermons as well as joining in choir selections through voice, hand claps, and tambourines. But this physical movement and audible celebration were not always welcomed. "When we were in the little church," recalled Cora Allen-Brown, "I was one of the first to play a tambourine. Sometimes people sitting near me would move because I played too loud."[29] This more explicit expression of praise was not the only one that yielded negative reactions. Brown was among others who "got happy" and "felt the spirit," to the dismay of many. "I didn't really care what people thought because I am not ashamed of praising God!" she explained. In later years, liturgical dance became an additional physical expression of praise as most members embraced embodied worship.

Trinity was also introduced to new ways of celebrating the black religious experience through the celebrations of Umoja Karamu, Kwanzaa, and the Watch Meeting Service. The first observance of Umoja Karamu, created by Dr. Edward Sims in 1971, was initially celebrated on Thanksgiving morning in 1975. It highlighted the solidarity of the black family through narration, music, and symbolic food. The second observance, beginning in 1974, was a churchwide celebration of the seven principles of Kwanzaa during the last week in December that featured presentations from various ministries, inviting the entire community to participate. The third observance was first celebrated at Trinity on New Year's Eve in 1972, in commemoration of the vigil of African slaves on December 31, 1862, of the anticipated freedom in 1863 through the Emancipation Proclamation. Through these worship experiences, this community of faith learned that the purpose of worship should not be restricted to Sunday or to the traditional liturgy alone but should provide opportunities to celebrate all aspects of life, including the joys and sorrows of being black and Christian.

No account of the Purpose at Trinity would be complete without attention to its emphasis on Christian education. Adult Bible study began in 1972 with one class following Wednesday prayer service taught by the pastor. "From the beginning," said Melbalenia D. Evans,[30] "Pastor Wright had the vision for Bible study being offered continuously at various levels. I was one of the first teachers and he empowered me to invite others to participate in providing instruction." Evans went on to be the first paid staff person to head the Bible Study Development Center, which by 1980 evolved into a series of biblical survey classes for adults. "We found that there was a burning hunger for knowledge of the Bible and God," she continued. "The Center was the direct result of Pastor Wright empowering lay leaders in the congregation to develop their gifts and subsequently use them to build the community of faith." It is important to note that Christian education was not restricted to Bible study for adults. It also included the work of all the ministries.

While these classes were considered regular and consistent settings for churchwide Christian education for adults, church school and Vacation Bible School (VBS) focused attention on the children, youth, and adults. While VBS took place two weeks during the summer, it was in the early 1980s that church school moved from its traditional spot on Sunday to Saturday morning. This major shift in time was a direct result of the addition of a second worship service that limited space for church school on Sundays. But it opened the way for an innovative approach in Christian education for children and youth that began with church school classes on Saturday morning and continued throughout the day with all other activities. Essentially, Christian education at Trinity expanded beyond the study of scripture for children, youth, and adults to include all forms of education that empowered members for service and greater witness.

As a congregation, Trinity now began to understand itself as being called by God for a Purpose that went beyond merely being proud of their social status but instead, required them to embrace the possibilities and recognize the value of bringing together their faith and their culture. Through this new perspective, Trinity was challenged to spread the gospel of Christ as well as to address the social, political, and economic issues that plagued the black community. More importantly it was called to a new concept of Purpose by actively participating in liberation as persons of African descent in America.

In the "Pastor's Statement" of the 1975 Annual Report, Pastor Wright wrote the following words that illustrated the early shift of this congregation in their Purpose:

> God has smiled on us and freed us up to be [God's] people—unshackled by stereotypes and the barriers of assimilation, unshackled by the fear of joining in the struggle for liberation, and unshackled by the stigmas, defeats, or victories of the past. [God] has freed us to be the Church in the world—[God's] Children! Black, Christian and proud of being created in [God's] image and being called by [God's] name.

Here he uses the metaphor of freedom to describe the journey from assimilation and fear to liberation and courage. What becomes clear in this statement is that Trinity's identity is not only one of being black but also one of being Christian. Hence, the freedom spoken of is not simply a matter of identity but also of affiliation, defining not only who they are but whose they are as it fortified their understanding of Purpose.

Also evident in the preceding quote is a new sense of Unity that linked the members of this congregation with their divine creator. Unfortunately, this did not always translate into Unity within the body of Christ. A crisis just as traumatic as the earlier one in the music ministry pointed directly to the issue of gender. From its inception, Trinity always looked to a group of self-appointed men who functioned as ushers. By the mid-1970s, however, there was a group of women who wanted to form a Women's Usher Board and share that responsibility with the men. Greatly disturbed by the very thought of such a change, one charter member vowed that there "would never be any women walking up and down the aisles as ushers at Trinity Church." Fortunately, this narrow perception was not shared by the majority, and the Women's Usher Board was instituted and combined with the men into one ministry. "This move was significant," recalled Wright, "because it paved the way for the full participation of women in every aspect of Trinity's life."

This acknowledgment of women became explicit with the ordination of Thanda Ngcobo, a native of South Africa and the first person to be ordained at Trinity, in 1975. She went on to be the director of Clinical Pastoral Education at the University of Chicago Hospitals and Clinics and was the first black woman to be certified by the Association of Clinical

Pastoral Education. Rev. Ngcobo's presence and accomplishments heightened the consciousness of many members of this congregation regarding issues of women in ministry, illustrating the diverse ways that women can serve. Following this historic moment in 1975, another came in 1979 with the ordination and installation of Barbara J. Allen as lay minister and assistant pastor. Rev. Allen began as a church school teacher who moved on to be the superintendent of the church school and later the director of Christian education. Admittedly, the next move to assistant pastor was "overwhelming" for her to say the least but in the process she said, "I was so grateful to be able to use my administrative skills in the church. I learned that being a minister is much more than preaching and that ministry is really an attitude that you receive when you recognize that you are called." The affirmation and support that she received by the members of Trinity point to another level of Unity that blurs the lines between lay and clergy and envisions ministry in a much broader and more inclusive way. It paved the way for the historic move that gave women the opportunity to serve as fully ordained deacons in 1980.

This ten-to-fifteen-year period marked a turning point in the church's focus on Unity as well as a new voice of Purpose. Expressions of black pride through worship and education and the inclusion of women in the life of the church were enhanced by forms of activism within the local church, the community, and the larger denomination. It was during this time that the Annual Report, for example, added "Black Witness in the UCC," to the table of contents. This was inspired by the increased involvement of Wright with the black caucuses of the UCC, Ministers for Racial and Social Justice (MRSJ), UBC and the Commission for Racial Justice (CRJ),[31] and his election as a member of CRJ. It increased the congregation's concern about and involvement in the social and political issues of the day, giving birth to a new and exciting sense of activism. In 1976 the Executive Council created the Church in Society (CIS) as one of its ad hoc committees that went on later to become a full ministry. The mission of this committee was dedicated to keeping "the church on the cutting edge insofar as issues, policies, legislation and so-called public sector matters that affect the lives of black people in our city, in our country, and in the world."[32]

Their most active involvement in this premier year involved the "Wilmington Ten." This historic case occurred initially in 1972 when

Rev. Benjamin Chavis, then director of the Washington, D.C., branch of the CRJ, was arrested in Wilmington, North Carolina, and convicted along with eight others[33] for fire bombing and conspiracy charges. In support of the Wilmington Ten and in connection with denominational efforts, CIS rallied the members of Trinity and other local UCC churches around a strong display of Purpose. Their efforts resulted in the filing of an amicus curie (friend of the court) brief that charged the state of North Carolina with constitutional violations, and in 1979 the Wilmington Ten were released.

This consolidation of energies and resources in addition to the aforementioned activities of the UBC created a solid black core within the UCC that could begin to accomplish what civil rights and integration failed to do. Once aware and confident of their identity as African Americans, the members of Trinity, hence, were further empowered to speak out in a purposeful response to injustices. They made no apologies to black nationalists of the day who questioned their commitment to the black cause because of their affiliation with a white denomination. They made no apologies to black Congregationalists, who chose to shun their connection to the idioms of the black religion tradition. They were not ashamed to speak out in a black, prophetic, Christian voice of Unity and Purpose.

One of the things that made Trinity's witness distinctive was that it was not simply grounded on a platform of Christian responsibility to feed the hungry, clothe the naked, and heal the sick. This congregation's evolving self-understanding was a renewed and more realistic consciousness that accepted the fact that black life in America, by design, also counted them in the numbers of the hungry, naked, and sick despite their "high potential" status. By adding a clear and often painful look at itself as an African American congregation, Trinity began to realize that no amount of social or educational achievement could erase the reality and result of racism on its life. Thus, through the combination of Unity of identity and Purpose of mission, this congregation could not continue to view God's divine mandate to feed, clothe, and heal in any other terms than through the lens of a theology of liberation.

Resisting the temptation of professing a black theology of separation or a white theology of homogeneity, the members of Trinity allowed their new theology of liberation to emerge out of an expanded awareness of Purpose and Unity as they attempted to serve faithfully as a community of faith. They were committed to a black cause that moved beyond the selfishness of classism and the euphoria of self-love to take on the harder task to love those who appeared to be unlike themselves, either black or white, and to include them in the struggle for liberation. God had truly brought the Trinity Church family a long way and had continued to smile on them. God freed them to be God's people in God's world and fashioned them into a church that would not be ashamed of their black heritage and one that would not apologize for their Christian faith.

It would be inaccurate, at this point, to imply that Trinity experienced uninterrupted Unity and undaunted Purpose as it grew from its small beginnings in 1961. The congregational efforts to build a consciously raised, prophetic church since 1972 suffered many moments of disappointment and loss. One was experienced following the initial thrusts toward black awareness in the early years of the 1970s. "When it became apparent that we were serious about trying to embrace and celebrate our African identity along with the Christian," said Wright, "twenty-two of the eighty-seven members who originally called me to the church moved to greener pastures. In most cases," he continued, "it was a reaction from members who would rather leave than fight the inevitable changes to come." In 1975, the second exodus took place when the Board of Deacons attempted to contact members who were visibly absent since the coming of the new pastor. That year, though ninety-four members joined, sixty-two transferred their membership or were simply taken off the rolls. Then in 1983, a smaller but more poignant exodus occurred when twenty-two active and prominent members left Trinity and the UCC for a local Pentecostal/Apostolic church whose teachings they found more compatible. While the loss of these twenty-two (five of whom returned) did not significantly depreciate the total membership (725 members joined that year), the incident illustrated that combining faith and culture was clearly not a priority for everyone. In the years that followed, Trinity, like most congregations, experienced the loss of members for a variety of reasons. Through it all, ongoing attempts were made to maintain a sense of Unity through an emphasis on the common threads of heritage and faith.

Opposition to the ministry and message of Trinity was not limited to its membership. The year 1978 revealed a painful example on the denominational level. In February of that year, a major conflict occurred between an Association official and Trinity Church. "It was instigated by members of the denomination (black and white) who misunderstood and disrespected the importance of the black religious experience and who were basically jealous," said Wright, "of Trinity's success." During the weeklong dedication services for the second new building, Trinity members were disappointed and perplexed when there were no official denominational representations at any part of this historic event. Aware of the growing tensions resulting from this incident, Conference Minister Cary called an impromptu session between Wright and the official. During this exchange, Trinity was accused of being a cult (only three months after Jim Jones and Jamestown!) and Wright of having an "ego problem." Fortunately, this situation was finally resolved through the reconciliatory efforts of a denominational task force and Trinity's Pastoral Relations Committee. It ended with an official apology from the denomination official but it bespeaks an unfortunate level of intolerance and disunity that opposes the very unity-in-diversity that the UCC was founded upon.

Despite the many costs of this emerging sense of Unity at Trinity, there were also many joys. "One of the greatest," said Wright, "was the lifelong friends that we acquired across racial and ecumenical lines over the years and the ability to share from the wealth of the black religious tradition with them, void of shame and apology." These relationships were born through intradenominational fellowship services with UCC churches, black and white, but also through opportunities to commune with sister churches across denominational lines, locally and nationally. They involved invitations accepted by or made for Trinity to participate in special churchwide celebrations. In most cases, it resulted in the transport of the pastor, the choir, and members across the city and even the country. These worship exchanges also spawned additional interactions between church fellowship groups and boards that linked congregations across regional and denominational lines.

Sunday, August 9, 1981, was another time for celebration in the life of Trinity that marked yet another shift in Trinity's enlarging sense of Purpose. On that day they honored one of their own, Dr. Manford Byrd, a charter member of Trinity and a prominent Chicago educator who was facing a major challenge in his career as the deputy superintendent of the school system. In an attempt to affirm him in the midst of his struggle, Trinity honored him in a special way with the institution of a scholarship in his name. In addition, Val Jordan, in conjunction with the Recognition Committee, worked to crystallize and publish what became known as the "Black Value System," in honor of Byrd. Originally attempting to model these values after the Ten Commandments, the committee finally expanded them to include the following twelve concepts:

+ Commitment to God
+ Commitment to the black community
+ Commitment to the family
+ Dedication to the pursuit of education
+ Dedication to the pursuit of excellence
+ Adherence to the black work ethic
+ Commitment to self-discipline and self-respect
+ Disavowal of the pursuit of "middle-classness"
+ Pledge to make the fruits of all developing and acquired skills available to the black community
+ Pledge to allocate regularly a portion of personal resources for strengthening and supporting black institutions
+ Pledge of allegiance to all black leadership who respond and embrace the system
+ Personal commitment to embracing the black value system

This value system was officially adopted by the congregation in 1981. "Its intent was to provide a parameter for all ministry foci and to be taught at every opportunity in the life of Trinity," said Jordan. It is important to note that it took several years for the congregational leaders to fully embrace and begin to incorporate these values into their ministry missions and foci. But the mere existence of such a value system illustrates Trinity's expanding sense of Purpose and Unity in its attempt to articulate values that would help to facilitate the link of their cultural identity with their faith.

By 1986, when Trinity celebrated its twenty-fifth anniversary it had over four thousand members,[34] two worship services each Sunday, and forty-four ministries supported administratively by twenty-three full-time paid staff members. At this point in its history, Trinity had become more comfortable being "Unashamedly Black and Unapologetically

Christian." There was a clearer understanding of the importance of Christian education from the black perspective and the celebration of the black religious experience in worship. The congregation was becoming more confident of its identity as black members of a mainline white denomination and there were a number of key leaders who actively participated in the work of the larger church. Its local outreach was more in touch with the community and more attuned to its major issues. And by this time, Trinity had also made the important steps of naming, embracing, and connecting key cultural values to its faith commitment.

The year 1988 marked the beginning of a third building campaign, and by the time they moved in 1994 the membership had grown to eight thousand. Like many culturally conscious megachurches of the time, Trinity was clearly black and proud. But their experiences and expressions of Unity and Purpose took yet another turn in the late 1980s and early 1990 as they began to overlap each other, helping this congregation begin the move from being "Unashamedly Black" to being more explicitly Africentric.

Because of numerous invitations to speak and minister outside of the United States, particularly in parts of the African Diaspora, Wright's connection with his African culture was deepened through the late 1980s, further expanding his own sense of self and causing a deeper interpretation of his faith to emerge. Being black and Christian took on new levels of importance as he shared in the lives and stories of persons of African descent all over the world. He discovered that despite the location, the same spirit of perseverance and faith, the same issues of identity and meaning, and the same quest for freedom and self-determination were shared throughout the world, wherever slavery, apartheid, colonialism, genocide, and other forms of racism were present. He discovered further that the gospel of liberation that sustained his forebears also empowered those of African descent in Brazil, Ghana, Honduras, Cuba, and the Ivory Coast. These experiences created a deeper sense of Unity that understood the importance of moving outside of a primary centeredness on the experiences of slavery in America to one that included common struggles of oppression in Africa and the Diaspora. But they forged a broader Purpose through a common heritage and worked to dismantle institutions of injustice and to build new institutions that would guarantee justice for all oppressed.

There was no way that Wright could keep this profound revelation to himself. He began initially sharing these insights in his sermons.[35] In the latter part of the 1980s and the beginning of the 1990s his preaching and teaching as well as the suggested reading for the congregation reflected his experiences. In the late 1980s, for example, there was a churchwide retreat focus on the *Karios Document*.[36] This theological treatise created by a group of multiracial lay and clergy leaders in South Africa condemned the oppression of apartheid and challenged the church to speak out in ways that would begin to dismantle this system. This study, though often challenging, awakened the members of Trinity to a struggle for liberation much like their own. It gave many a more global perspective on the presence of oppression and a stronger conviction to join the struggle on behalf of all oppressed. During this time the word "apartheid" and the names Winnie and Nelson Mandela became an active part of the conversations, thoughts, and prayers of this congregation, even the youth and children.

The area of Bible study was also affected by the subtle but important shift toward Africentricity. In 1992, the administration began to understand its Purpose in a new way as it decided to change the name of the Bible Study Development Center to the Center for African Biblical Studies. "Our goal was to consistently reflect the emerging emphasis on our African heritage in light of the biblical tradition," said Deacon Shirley Bims-Ellis, director. "What was preached in the pulpit was taught in the classroom and sold in the bookstore,"[37] she added. The classes, consequently, included a focus on the African origins of Christianity, the African presence in the Bible, and use of maps to provide a visual connection between the stories in the Bible and the geographic connection to the continent of Africa. The church school followed in this vein in its continued commitment to provide curriculum that was more culturally relevant. "We have always struggled to find materials that were biblically and culturally grounded," said Frances D. Harris, church school superintendent.[38] "Because very few resources fit that requirement, we found it necessary to 'tweak' the curricular resources that we used in ways that effectively combined our African and biblical heritages." In each of these examples, the selection/creation of African-centered materials was supported by ongoing teacher training, which introduced the concepts of African-centered teaching and learning.[39]

Another very important part of this move toward Africentricity was the intentional exposure of the congregation to key scholars from a variety of disciplines. From the area of black psychology came Bobby Wright, Wade Nobles, and Na'im Akbar. Biblical scholars included Latta Thomas, Clarice Martin, Randall Bailey, and Cain Hope Felder. From the field of theology came Henry and Ella Mitchell, Dwight Hopkins, and Gayraud Wilmore and Cornel West with critical social and philosophical commentary. Additionally, Jake Carruthers brought insights from Kemetic studies, and Molefa Asante with an Afrocentric perspective. During regularly scheduled workshops, lectures, and seminars, these scholars helped the congregation to understand more clearly the gifts and challenges of being Christians of African descent who live and witness in America.

This gaze toward Africa was seen in other ways as ministries began to change their names to reflect the new understanding of their connectedness to Africa. The Special Citizens ministry, which provided support and nurture for members with special physical needs, for instance, changed its name to Kugichagulia. "The attendance and participation of the ministry at Kwanzaa each year," said Aletta Jumper, one of the founders, "influenced us to reflect on our African identity, and the definition of Kugichagulia (self-determination) became very important to us. This ministry, through its name change, gave the congregation a lived example of self-determination through members who may be seen by many as "special" or different, as the ministry moved to be instrumental in it outreach to all people."[40] In a similar way, other ministries made name changes. The Young Adult Choir, for example, chose Imani Ya Watume, meaning "Messengers of Faith," as the singers began to understand their ministry in song as a way to spread the gospel. The male and female mentoring programs went from "Building Black Men" and "Building Black Women" to Isuthu and Intonjane, meaning "Moving into Manhood" and "Moving into Womanhood," respectively. These examples reveal the simultaneous broadening of Unity and the deepening of Purpose as this congregation began to move closer to an African-centered identity.

One of the most formative experiences of this congregation that clearly helped it to acknowledge and embrace stronger ties with Africa came in the form of face-to-face encounters with sisters and brothers from the African continent and throughout the Diaspora. In addition to the presence of Rev. Thanda Ngobo and educational experiences of the choirs with Dr. Elkin T. Sithole,[41] a South African musicologist in the 1970s, Trinity's growing membership also included a large and active number of persons from the Caribbean. Through their presence, the congregation was exposed to the cultures in this part of the Diaspora through the Caribbean Connection, a ministry that began in 1978. The first cultural gift from this ministry was an awareness of the diversity found in the Caribbean. Claiming members from Jamaica, Haiti, Belize, Puerto Rico, Panama, and elsewhere, this ministry opened a new world of art, music, and cuisine to the members of Trinity during the annual Caribbean Festivals and other activities throughout the year. It clearly dispelled the miseducated assumption that all Caribbeans are Jamaican and that the only contribution from that part of the world is reggae music. It is also important to note that the cultural diversity of Trinity also extends to include about twenty-five to thirty continental Africans as active members in recent years.

In light of the wider exposure and growing numbers, the Purpose of this congregation was informed by its new identity and empowered by its prophetic voice to speak a word about what it really meant to be "Unashamedly Black and Unapologetically Christian." This emerging sense of Purpose that had an outward thrust in the 1980s was an advancement over the earlier, more parochial emphasis on local ministry of the 1970s. During its years of struggle to be both black and Christian, Trinity began to add the responsibility to equally balance its efforts to strengthen its local congregation with a serious concern for the larger community. This overlapping of ministry and mission became at once an "outreach" and an "inreach" where the local ministries were missions within themselves that nurtured and prepared their members for greater service in the community and the world. Through a holistic thrust that combined the heart, head, and will, Trinity was empowered with a new Purpose: one that included the local congregation, the black community, and the larger society.

Dr. Iva Carruthers, a member of the Long-Range Planning Ministry, reflected on the impact of Trinity's efforts to connect with Africa. "Despite these direct and personal exposures within the congregation to the African Diaspora," she commented, "it was our ministry to the village of Saltpond in Ghana that opened the way for this congregation to see, touch, and experience Africa."[42] By the 1990s Trinity had supported the efforts of the Saltpond Redevelopment Institute (SRI) financially for over a decade.

Founded in 1981 and acquiring not-for-profit status in 1986, SRI had as its mission the revitalization of the economic and human condition of Saltpond, Ghana, West Africa. The plan was to help the town "maintain and preserve local traditional values and systems with the help of the elderly and the rebirth in the youth," said Carruthers. With a population of fifteen thousand, this township was the center for the liberation movement in that region during the 1940s and '50s. In addition to direct financial contributions, Trinity combined its efforts with others to provide a back-up generator and to install two water reservoirs for the hospital in Saltpond. "In 1998," stated Carruthers, "we collaborated with SRI to create the Saltpond Institute of Technology, which provided computer access for the community, including an eleven-station computer network, sixty educational programs, and satellite hookup." Despite several setbacks, the facility was completed and dedicated in August 2000. A number of Trinity members were in attendance, and they brought blankets, shoes, and clothing for the hospital. Muriel Thompson, one of the members, summed up the impact of this experience when she said, "I felt blessed and empowered by the spirit of both giving and receiving. I realize, more than ever, my connection and responsibility to the Motherland."[43]

Throughout the 1990s, a number of trips were taken to Saltpond, providing opportunities for members to witness the result of their outreach efforts and to help them move toward greater levels of Unity and deeper experiences of Purpose. These trips inspired the creation of the Africa Ministry. In an attempt at preventing the visits from being seen as a vacation, shopping spree, or holiday, the leadership of this ministry took intentional strides to craft these trips as Christian education sojourns to Africa. "Our major goals," said Patricia Eggleston, founder of the Africa Ministry, "was to enhance the congregation's Africentric identity, to increase their awareness of the joys and concerns of Africa, [and] to provide opportunities for dialogue with African Christians as well as collaboration that supports empowered institutions in Africa."

Advanced preparation for these "sojourns" was required and it included workshops that centered on the people and culture. It also included daily classes during the trip as well as debriefing about the experiences and reflections upon return to Chicago. In addition to scheduling times of worship and fellowship between host and visitors, there were also special trips to the slave castles and the current churches in those slave castles where their slave ancestors awaited transport during the trans-Atlantic slave trade. By taking this approach, members were provided an opportunity to reconnect with their past while building relationships with those on the African continent. Additional trips were also taken to South Africa, Ethiopia, Senegal, Cote d'Ivoire, and Brazil to teach the diversity of the continent and its cultures. Although each trip averaged thirty-five to forty people, the cost of this experience was clearly not within the reach of most members. "Over the years," said Wright, "we have been intentional about limiting the number of trips to keep the cost within range." It was, however, through the efforts of the Africa Ministry that the impact of the trips was actualized for the many who could not travel to Africa. Their collaborative work with others on behalf of African countries, their ongoing education about Africa within the congregation, and their continued liaison with the Saltpond village helped to prepare this congregation for a stronger sense of Unity and a more focused sense of Purpose as they approached the twenty-first century.

Because storytelling in a congregational setting truly affirms identity and gives purpose and meaning to existence, as stated earlier by Roof, this narrative snapshot of Trinity UCC can help "sharpen our sensitivities" as we discover the ways that Unity and Purpose are embodied in this congregation's life and ministry. This congregational story, however, cannot be separated from the historical context of the 1960s and 1970s, introduced through the recollections of an adolescent girl, Romney Payne, and the memories of a middle-aged man, S. L. Allen. The former searched for Unity and a way to make sense of her world, while the latter sought ways to improve the quality of life for his family and to reestablish Purpose in his own life. In both cases, they found the church as a place that affirmed who they were and provided a sense of both meaning and belonging. These renewed insights fortified their religious commitments and became the catalyst for their ministry passion within Trinity United Church of Christ as they attempted to walk the talk and keep the faith.

WALKIN' THE TALK OF UNITY AND PURPOSE
Unity

This principle was always an important value in the life of Trinity UCC and, during its early years, the primary quest for it was through the experience of integration. It is important to remember that Trinity was founded only seven years after the landmark *Plessy versus Ferguson* decision of the Supreme Court of 1896 was overturned by the *Brown versus the Board of Education of Topeka Kansas* decision of 1954, declaring that racially segregated public schools were unconstitutional. The ruling set into motion a chain reaction that began to topple many inequitable barriers in society. This historic event was particularly relevant in a northern city like Chicago where segregation was as alive as it was in the South. Many early Trinity members spent their formative years living in the Black Belt of the South and West side of the city and attending segregated schools. This court ruling gave hope beyond education. These families could now move beyond the designated boundaries and live anywhere that they pleased. This court ruling made Trinity's new membership as a black congregation in a mainline white denomination an important step forward in the goal of integration and an expression of Unity in stark contrast to the practices and experiences of segregation.

In those earlier days, when the members of Trinity viewed their identity in terms of this social reality, some felt they had to choose between being black (or in those days, Negro) and being Christian. In light of the ideology of the day, the banner of Christian held more inclusive and universal value for them, so their identity as Congregationalists who *happened* to be black was a significant statement. Their membership in this denominational family decisively shaped the contours of both meaning and belonging, developing values and dictating what congregational life should be. They placed a high regard on the denominationally designated status as "high potential" because of their tendency to be more like other white UCC congregations. This attitude created what St. Claire Drake and Horace R. Cayton in the book *Black Metropolis* called a "class gulf" between middle- and lower-class churches.[44] Trinity's efforts to maintain Unity around their social status distinguished them from lower-class churches, primarily as a reaction to the emotional behavior exhibited in worship by these religious fellowships. Their tendency to value more highly their connection to white Congregationalism not only separated them from some of their black sisters and brothers but also from a part of the black religious experience that many knew about but chose to forget.

This understanding of Unity resembled Karenga's traditional description in that its focus was narrow and exclusive. Unity of family, community, and race for Karenga was unashamedly restricted to the African Diaspora. Trinity's notion of Unity in a similar way pulled together across very exclusive lines of class and denominational affiliation. They both responded to the realities of racism in America with expressions of separation and exclusivity—Karenga with separation of the African race from non-Africans and Trinity with a separation across lines of denomination and class. While Karenga's position of Unity has a clear motivation of solidarity of black people against racism, Trinity's was more complex, for it suggested not simply a separation between groups of people but a bifurcation of the very identity of that people. But in each case, the primary focus was on sociology rather than theology; that is, Unity was seen as a horizontal transaction with little vertical accountability. But as their consciousness began to shift, inspired by a new look at themselves through the lens of faith, a restated definition of Unity began to emerge for Trinity—*to seek and maintain a relationship with God that affirms our connection to Africa and calls forth solidarity among and liberation for all of God's people.* They began to understand that the "shared identity" was multidimensional and could cross the boundaries of race, class, gender, and region. They could be black, middle-income, and a part of the UCC as long as their core rootedness was shaped and directed by a God of liberation and justice.

When the dimension of faith is added, and the locus of all Unity is recentered and anchored in God, the entire focus is broadened. A genuine relationship with God calls forth a mandate of solidarity and harmonious relationship with others. For Trinity, this solidarity began with togetherness among African peoples before it could go on to acts of liberation for all of God's people. It is important to emphasize, at this point, that this concept of self departs from an Africentric notion that, in the words of Na'im Akbar, "must begin by understanding the universe as a Divine Creation and to see ourselves as a part of a Divine drama."[45] This orientation of self becomes the basis for what he calls a tribal identity that "identifies the collective historical and shared experiences that have shaped us in the particular form that we are."[46] He is quick to note that this notion of self does not imply a level of superiority over others but provides instead a space to acknowledge and appreciate "unique and special gifts," that have not historically been acknowledged. Consequently, a Unity for Trinity that begins with acceptance of African peoples among themselves provides a strong platform for their continued interaction with others.

Finally, this talk about Unity and solidarity is only made real when it is allowed it to be domesticated by the necessity of risk. Remaining exclusively in the realm of family, community, and race or social class and denomination can be comforting and affirming but it can also produce values that reinforce, overtly or covertly, categories of superiority and inferiority. There is a risk, however, when we step outside of those comfort zones and attempt to enter into relationships with the "other" that may result in change on our part. Talking about Unity is one thing but walking that talk in light of our expanded description is another. It brings together culture and faith, people of African and non-African descent, and presents a formidable challenge for congregations that self-identify as African-centered. The key, however, to a workable union between the two is acknowledging that the ultimate power comes from God and that the concrete result is seen in responsible and accountable engagement in the community through an African-centered spirituality.

Purpose

The Purpose of anything refers to its intent, its aim, its reason to be, and Trinity's Purpose has always been one of religious commitment as seen in their worship and faithful service as disciples of Christ. This Purpose was lived out in many ways and during the early years, it was summed up in the motto, "In the heart of the community ever seeking to win the community's heart." This statement in the most general terms identified this congregation as a church that was committed to doing the work of God in its community but it also extended its mission to include faithful participation in the denomination. Their role in the community as an institution that sought love, support, and respect is very close to Karenga's original description of Purpose. Both affirmed them as they were heirs and custodians in their respective legacies; however, Trinity's legacy aligned itself more with America and her commitment to democracy than Africa and her expression of communality. Both Karenga and Trinity embraced a Purpose, "committed to a collective vocation." For Karenga it was "to restore [African] people to their traditional greatness." For Trinity, in the early days, it was to live in the fullness of a "high potential" church and be an example to Christians everywhere, regardless of color.

A shift in the Purpose of this congregation became apparent, however, with the writing of the congregational job description in the shadow of its declining membership and its uncertain future. In the words of this document, Trinity desired to move from simply being a faithful community church to being a "source of spiritual sustenance, security and inspiration, [and serving] as instrument of God and church in [their] communities and the world . . ." While the words, "racism" and "oppression," were never used, it is clear that this congregation was aware of and opposed to their presence in society that contributed to the "dehumanization of persons [that] perpetuates their psychological enslavement." This statement signaled a move toward activism that could challenge unjust systems and aligns with the restated definition: *to build and develop our communities in ways that acknowledge the sacredness of our collective work of liberation in the Diaspora and the world and our dependence on God's power and grace to perform it.*

A noteworthy observation is that this document was not for the new pastor but for the congregation itself, pointing to an emerging awareness of the sacredness of collective work. Through it, Trinity expressed the desire to move toward an intentionally communal ownership of the task at hand. This was indeed a step toward "seeking to win the community's heart." Through this congregational job description, we see a move from a more insular congregational agenda toward an expanded Purpose—the collective work of building and developing their church and community as a sacred act that finds its strength and direction in the power and grace of God. They received a new understanding of their role as "instruments of God and the church" in the community and the world. With the very thoughtful and intentional inclusion of a faith dimension, Purpose speaks to a broader reality that asks difficult questions, challenges opposing perspectives, and gives a glimpse of an emergent Africentric spirituality.

Trinity continued to broaden its congregational Purpose to include a growing sense of black pride. The adoption of the affirmation "Unashamedly Black and Unapologetically Christian," added a clear awareness of its communal responsibility and a desire to boldly unite culture and faith, replacing their earlier posture of separating the two. This new affirmation did not replace their original motto but moved it toward a more solid theological grounding and a more spiritual intentionality. Their notion of faith was deeper than a traditional alignment with a denomination and their understanding of culture was closer than a sociological connection to a community. At this point Trinity began to understand the possibility as well as the necessity of bringing faith and culture together.

This slow but sure shift in consciousness at Trinity was in sharp contrast to the general decline in black churches across the nation at that time. Anthony E. Pinn, in *The Black Church in the Post–Civil Rights Era,* says this national shift occurred because of "the end of the civil rights movement and the rise of more radical and nationalistic orientations [that] brought into question the merit of church involvement."[47] A large part of Trinity's ability to reimagine their original Purpose and resist the kind of apathy that was present in many black churches of the time was due to its ongoing commitment to justice that was continually informed and supported by the commitments of the UCC. It was also a result of the further development of their Purpose toward a perspective more grounded in a theological conviction, and their emerging sense of Purpose found its locus in a God of love. This love was made particular in that it mandated them to love themselves as persons of African descent. This new formed self-love was further supported by the Black Value System they claimed that challenged them to shed the garment of "middle-classness" with its rugged individualism and opted instead for values that reflected a more communal way of life. It also presented the difficult task of humbly acknowledging God's all-powerful and active presence in the life of the faith community in lieu of relying exclusively on the strength of human status and accomplishments. It acknowledged their emerging African-centered legacy that was sustained by God's power and grace. Finally, it signaled a visionary move that not only redefined their direction but also proactively stepped forward to accept the responsibility to be more decisive in their plans and more purposeful in their actions as they moved toward embracing an African-centered spirituality.

five

Keepin' the Faith in a Congregational Context

Faith

THROUGHOUT THE LAST THREE CHAPTERS, Imani Temple Christian Fellowship, First Afrikan Presbyterian Church, and Trinity United Church of Christ have been viewed through the lenses of particular principles that revealed their efforts toward linking faith and culture. It is important to note that while this discussion highlighted specific values for each congregation, additional time and space could have expanded the discussion to show all principles at work in each congregation. From our brief glimpse, it is also obvious that certain principles could have clearly had much more emphasis than others. But in each case, the expressions of the principles went beyond being simply nice things to do. They became spiritual practices that provided a foundation for each congregation's mission and ministry. With that thought in mind, this chapter will look at Faith as the common principle that links the other six together and that makes the vital connection to an emergent Africentric spirituality.

The dictionary defines faith as "unquestioning belief that does not require proof and evidence; belief in God, religious tenets, etc." Hebrews 11:1 concurs as it states that faith is the "assurance of things hoped for, the conviction of things not seen." It then goes on to highlight women and men in biblical history that showed "unquestioning belief" and abiding trust in God. For many, this sends a very clear message—the duty of Christians is to express faith in God. As basic as it is, this conclusion does not take into consideration the realities of church life and the various ways that Faith is defined and lived in a congregational context. In other words, it does not give witness to the transformative dimension of faith.

There is, for example, faith in the tradition. The be-all and end-all of some congregational ministries and missions is to have an abiding faith in the inherited programs, politics, and polity of their denomination. Whether Baptist, Methodist, Pentecostal, Episcopalian, or Lutheran, many congregations unashamedly proclaim faith in the history and heritage of their respective ecclesiastical bodies and they interpret it, broadly, as having faith in God. The denomination is historically the institutional vehicle through which God has proclaimed an abiding presence in the world throughout the centuries, but what they fail to realize is that belief in this institution alone is not enough. There is also a tendency for other churches to claim their ultimate faith in the Bible. They proudly proclaim faith in the literal, infallible Word of God. The framework of all they say and do in ministry is based on knowing the Word of God and they interpret this knowing as faith in God. Certainly the Bible is the mysterious Word of God that transcends time and space as well as human tendencies and situations to speak today as it did yesterday, but what they forget is that belief in the Bible alone in not enough. Still for others there is faith in the pastor. These congregations passionately embrace the vision of a particular leader. Their involvement is based on a strong commitment to his/her ministry and they interpret this commitment as faith in God. The pastor is indeed the anointed servant of God whose prophetic utterances and teachings announce the coming of God's realm on earth, but what they ignore is that belief in the vision of an anointed leader alone is not enough. In each example, congregations unconsciously worship their tradition, the Bible, or their pastor, and in so doing transfer their ultimate faith from God to those things and people inspired by God. There is, consequently a danger in understanding and experiencing faith as simply the act of believing that leads to an idolatrous expression of ministry and mission that creates barriers to real individual and societal transformation.

There is another defining variation of faith, however, found in James 2:17 that says, "faith by itself, if it has no works, is dead." Faith in this way is not simply belief but belief put into action. This does not mean that works prove faith but that faith inspires works and is strengthened by grace. For these three congregations, this notion of Faith translates into "doing theology" informed by Unity, Self-Determination, Collective Work and Responsibility, Cooperative Economics, Purpose, and Creativity. Note that this "doing theology" takes place quite well without explicit claims to Africentricity. Many congregations draw from these key principles in ways that produce vital and transforming ministry. Within the three congregations profiled, however, there is another dimension of doing theology that centers on orientation and location. Christianity for them is a faith experience in light of the reality of life in the African Diaspora and their mission and ministries reflect a radical reinterpretation of that faith while in exile. This perspective broadens the scope of ministry but more importantly it identifies a centering place—a home.

For these contemporary congregations, the origin of Christianity finds its home in Africa. It yields a spirituality that connects them geographically, historically, biblically, and ancestrally as a people of exile. They acknowledge the establishment of the first African church in 42 C.E. by the Cyrenian Jew John Mark, who was also the companion of Paul and the author of the second gospel. They celebrate the planting of Christianity in the Upper Nile Valley by Judich, the Ethiopian eunuch spoken of in Acts 8:36–40 and the later adoption of Christianity in Ethiopia by the fourth century. They are also aware of the solid presence of Christianity among the native Copts of Egypt and the strength of their church.[1] Through this knowledge they have denounced the notion that Christianity is the "white man's religion" as they celebrate its African origins. They acknowledge their physical disconnection from that place of beginnings and seek ways to reconnect and find wholeness. Through this Diaspora consciousness, they find wholeness as they unite with the history and heritage of Africa as well as with its people—their estranged sisters and brothers. This reconnecting, consequently, is not simply across land and space but also across time and cultures. They must figure out how to honor who they are by virtue of creation with who they are becoming in Christ. They must learn how to sing God's song in a strange land.

It is important to recognize that the key for them is not simply identifying with Africa but seriously considering what it means to be a people of the Christian faith as a part of the African Diaspora. To insist on being both African and Christian in America then is to live in the midst of a historic tension complicated by the need to survive amid captivity, slavery, and Jim/"Jane" Crow but encouraged by the hope to thrive despite it all. This requires a peculiar understanding of Faith that must be Christ-rooted. It must completely embrace a gospel that speaks of redemption and salvation in the life to come as well as reconciliation and liberation in this one. This Faith must also be African-centered. It is essential that it begins with an acknowledgment of Africa in all its richness and challenge but also examines and reappropriates values and perspectives that support the building of God's realm on earth for all of God's creation.

With this in mind, the definition of Faith has been restated so that it aligns with the other six principles and reflects this reality—*to always look to and depend upon the presence and power of the reconciling and liberating spirit of God that transforms what we say, do, think, and dream beyond our imagination for the benefit of all creation.* This understanding of Faith is not simply believing in oneself or believing in God, although it requires the partnership of both. The key here is the desire and ability to embrace God's power in Faith and then become willing instruments of God that will transform individuals and society. This transformation cannot be conceived of as a magic, automatic change but one that comes through struggle and even failure. This transformation is no different in its experience from that of those who have gone on before, and for these congregations, Faith in this transformation provides a way to survive as well as thrive.

In light of the emergent theology of exile introduced by Roberts earlier, these congregations each believe that real transformation only happens when they resist being stuck in a survival mode and step out in Faith to discover ways to thrive by doing theology. Through their respective ministries and missions, they have made genuine efforts to keep the Faith in a congregational context.

IMANI TEMPLE CHRISTIAN FELLOWSHIP

Four years is a very short time in the life of a congregation, yet in this brief period, Imani Temple has laid the foundation for a ministry of healing and fellowship through experiences of restoration and community. Through the bifocal lenses of Collective Work/Responsibility and Creativity we saw Imani take the first-century church experience of *koinonia* and translate it into a relevant experience of community for twenty-first-century African Americans. Both principles in their renewed forms suggest a theology of liberation as seen in Jesus' words in Luke 4:18–19, "the spirit of the Lord is upon me, because he has anointed me to bring the good news to the poor. He has sent me to proclaim release to the captives and recovery of sight to the blind, to let the oppressed go free, to proclaim the year of the Lord's favor." The activities of proclaiming, preaching, and restoring are found at the heart of Imani's ministry commitment. They find strength and motivation rooted in the resurrection power of Christ and centered on the problems and promises of being Christians of African descent in America. Ultimately, liberation for Imani is found in the Word of God that makes all things new. For this congregation, all things include the realities of life in the Inland Empire of southern California where many experience geographical isolation and community fragmentation. Restoration that comes from this liberation finds its most healing balm in the midst of community where the pain of one becomes the pain of all *and* the restorative healing of one promises healing for all. This is an invaluable ingredient for a people attempting to move from surviving to thriving in a contemporary life of exile.

This has been the experience in countless encounters of Imani and the member churches of COPE as they gathered over the past four years around the issues of their communities. The return of ex-prisoners into the Inland Empire, for example, without the necessary skills to create personal meaning and make valuable contributions to the community is not a problem of an individual alone but a responsibility of the community. Despite their commitment to disassociate with traditional denominational structures and polity, Imani found in the ecumenical gathering of COPE a broader sense of accountability and a more abundant pool of resources than they would as a single congregation.

Imani was also willing to share the corporate pain in the hope of a corporate restoration that benefits all. Their effort to be grounded in a communal spirit sketches the contours of an African-centered spirituality that says, "I am because we are."

Imani's experiences of outreach in the Inland Empire through COPE are not unlike those in other churches. This kind of ministry, in many contemporary congregations, resembles the efforts of the social gospel movement in the early twentieth century. During these years, many Protestant churches adopted a socially sensitive outreach and understood it as a moral response to the economic and social crises of the day, as they sought to bring about justice in society. It is, moreover, in a similar spirit that congregations create and implement programs of outreach today, as they identify the anomalies in society and try to make meaningful changes. The downside of this experience is that it often takes the form of programs and activities that are *reaction* rather than *proaction*. They seek a temporary solution for an immediate need without necessarily addressing the systemic nature of the originating oppression. Outreach as a *proactive* response, on the other hand, is keenly aware that unless institutional issues are also addressed, the efforts will be superficial at best. This kind of response ideally begins by establishing a relationship between all involved so that through dialogue, joint decisions are made, cooperative strategies are designed, and all grow in grace from the experience.

This is indeed what happened as Imani and the other COPE congregations dialogued with government officials as well as the families of the incarcerated and with teachers, administrators, and parents, to forge a viable plan of action. In both COPE educational initiatives described earlier, the proactive route was to get to the root of the problem. For Frisbee it extended beyond elevating low test scores to elevating a sense of self-worth and hope in the students. For the GED program it went beyond referrals to minimum wage jobs after release from prison to providing the educational and motivational tools to think about and be prepared for a career. The goal in each case was a win/win result that would heal individuals, communities, and institutions.

I suggest that Imani's experience of outreach, seen through the restated lenses of Collective Work/Responsibility and Creativity and undergird by Faith, has a sacramental quality. By definition, a sacrament is "an outward sign instituted by God to convey an inward or spiritual grace," as in the celebration of baptism and communion in Protestant churches. Both invite believers to share in the joy of knowing a divine love that reconciles them to their God and to each other. As Imani extends its time and resources to aid and assist those in need, it has potential for overcoming estrangement and creating a space for healthy relationships. This is of particular significance given the isolation and fragmentation in the Inland Empire across racial, class, and geographic lines. In the spirit of Collective Work/Responsibility and Creativity, this invites genuine fellowship.

Through Faith it becomes a sacramental act of reconciliation and restoration that is grounded in the love of God and genuine concern for the community at large. The experiences of the men at Frisbee Middle School, for example, could have been the more traditional exchange between mentor and mentee where the former instructs, informs, and shapes the latter. While there was a definite experience of the older guiding the younger, the experience took on a sacramental quality as the men soon saw themselves in a different light because of their experiences with the young boys. They realized that if they were to give a lasting impression that would bring healing and hope, their walk would have to match their talk. In the process of being a mentor, these men were transformed as they experienced God's grace through a deeper level of spiritual energy and vitality, expanding their experience of spirituality.

Peter Paris, in his book *The Spirituality of African Peoples: The Search for a Common Moral Discourse,* defines spirituality as "the dynamic and integrative power that constitutes the principle frame of meaning for individual and collective experiences.[2] He is quick to point out that this power is rooted in the soul. "Metaphorically," he says, "the spirituality of a people is synonymous with the soul of a people."[3] Spirituality in this understanding begins with ontology or the reality of being rather than action. But this ontological location is only the beginning. It is further expressed and lived out, for Paris, through the "dynamic structural unity among the four constitutive spheres of African experiences, namely: God, community, family and person."[4] For Paris, the spirituality of African peoples begins with the reality of the soul in all its animating and integrating potential but finds actualization in the context of community. Imani's experience of outreach illustrates this sense of community that provided the space for growth and healing. When faced with the ontological realities of southern California life, this convicting spirit animates action through both individual and corporate efforts for the sake of individual and collective wholeness. Herein lie the emerging contours of an African-centered spirituality. It is grounded in the kind of community consciousness that begins with being but finds its fullest expression through communal action and commitment.

Through outreach experiences of a sacramental quality, this congregation is learning that it is not about them. It is not about those who are helped. It is about recognizing the grace-filled gifts that God bestows upon all. In this way, it becomes both the receiver and the giver in the outreach experience, all because of the knowledge that God's love is the link that brings it all together. Attempting to view these experiences through the renewed lenses of Collective Work/Responsibility and Creativity informed by Faith provides the members of Imani with clues that lead to a deeper sense of Africentric spirituality. The desired outcome is that they recognize the value of balancing their being and their doing in ways that reinforce community and encourage restoration as they strive to keep the faith in the congregational context.

FIRST AFRIKAN PRESBYTERIAN CHURCH

For a decade, FAPC slowly named and claimed itself as an Africentric community of faith in a political, economic, and social ethos of transition. Its story uncovered a steady, sometimes challenging journey to clarify this identity as its numbers increased and its ministries expanded. This congregation finds its physical home in a city hailed as the Mecca of the southeast due to recent growth, development, and prosperity. It finds its ecclesial home within the Presbyterian Church, USA, which seeks to contextualize the gospel through a mission that is "biblically based and historically appropriate."[5] In the midst of a burgeoning metropolis and a reformed church they embrace traditions shaped by their African past that result in new expressions of ministry for the future. As we view their story through the lenses of Self-Determination and Cooperative Economics, supported by Faith, we see a portrait of an African American congregation that honors tradition as it seeks innovation.

Echoing Proverbs 29:18a they truly believe that "where there is no vision the people will perish (KJV)," which is seen in the sentiments of the theme song they sing each Sunday, "Building Beyond Our Years."

This congregation has indeed caught a radical vision, informed by the past in anticipation of the future. Cooperative Economics and Self-Determination present a twofold meaning in their metaphor of "building." Through the first, there is the vision of physical structures and enduring institutions that support the congregation and community as they move from surviving to thriving. Through the second, there is a call to deconstruct and reconstruct the individual and collective self in ways that embrace and embody both culture and faith.

An illustrative example of how these principles appear in this congregation is through their adoption of the alternative liturgical calendar described earlier. As with the traditional Christian calendar, their church year is divided into four seasons, each with an accompanying color. The genius of this alternative liturgical calendar is that it interweaves the theological movements of the Christian faith into the cultural rhythms of the African American community. In the first quarter, for example, it finds rootedness in the promise of redemption and reconciliation with God during Lent and Easter, as it also finds centeredness in a cultural reality that relates to the experience of Birth. In this context, February ceases to be a time to acknowledge and rehearse African American history in a narrow sense and becomes instead the celebration of African Liberation Month in a more global sense. This gives birth to a new orientation that does not begin four hundred years ago with slavery in America but extends back over five thousand years,[6] acknowledging the legacy of the ancient African continent.

During the spring and the traditional season of Pentecost, the liturgical emphasis moves to a celebration of Life with a focus on family and freedom. Mother's Day and Father's Day are more than opportunities to acknowledge parenthood. Together they embrace the importance of relationality through kinship ties and name the extended family as a viable norm for sustaining community. Juneteenth,[7] as the oldest known celebration of the ending of slavery, claims the promises of freedom. These promises extend beyond individual liberation and mandate the use of all available resources empowered by the spirit, for the life and freedom of the entire community.

The third season that parallels the traditional emphasis on "ordinary time" is far from ordinary through its focus on New Afrikan Consciousness and Caribbean Liberation. Within this season of

Transformation, FAPC names and claims an awareness of and commitment to the larger Diaspora. Through a historical, cultural, and spiritual consciousness of the Diaspora, this bond opens the way for transformation of the mundane into the extraordinary, inspired by God's abiding presence that transcends time and space, in ways that connects them historically, culturally, and spiritually. Finally, aligning with the celebration of Advent are the high days of Emancipation Sunday, Zawadi Emphasis, Ancestral Remembrance Week, Kwanzaa Series, and Umoja Karamu. This season of Return marks an ending as well as a beginning. It celebrates simultaneously the coming of Christ as the incarnation and the enduring presence of the ancestors as it names and claims the nonlinear reality of both the African and biblical world.[8]

During each of these seasons of the liturgical year, the members of FAPC flex their muscles of Self-Determination as they continue to name their reality. This in turn gives them the confidence and strength to claim their destiny through Cooperative Economics as they make use of human, spiritual, intellectual, and material resources in ministry. Together these principles lay the foundation for an Africentric spirituality that links the past with the present and is grounded in Faith.

Self-Determination and Cooperative Economics are also quite apparent in this congregation's contemporary expression of a black Christian nationalism. In line with Cleage's belief in the potential institutional power of a revolutionary black church, FAPC names and claims its political voice that speaks a prophetic message of liberation. Both Cleage and FAPC affirm the reorganization and restructure of the resources within the black church and community for liberation, informed and inspired by Jesus Christ of Nazareth, the black Messiah. Cleage, however, criticized the black church of the 1960s for its choice to focus more on the destiny of black people in the hereafter rather than addressing their powerlessness in this world.[9] He rejected the idea of the black church as a strong and potent institution because it "does not exist to serve the power interest of the black people." The remedy, in his eyes, was the creation of the Shrine of the Black Madonna and other institutions and structures within the black community to establish and support "a nation within a nation."[10]

But while Cleage stressed the harnessing of political, social, and economic power through separation, FAPC conceives of it through coalition. Their work with Atlantans Building Leadership for Empowerment (ABLE), for example, combines the efforts of twenty-seven congregations of various religious traditions toward the goal of adequate housing for all in Atlanta. Together they are committed to bringing about political, economic, and social change in tangent with business and government. This involvement is a key part of their First Afrikan Community Development Corporation goal to establish a partnership for revitalization and development in the community and illustrates both Self-Determination and Cooperative Economics. It is important to note that this coalition does not diminish their sense of connectedness to Africa and the Diaspora or to Faith. This congregation relies on the spiritual power and presence of the Afrikan Messiah in their midst, who at once reminds them where they have been and charts the path for where they should go. They are encouraged by the biblical story of black Hebrews who were able to retain a sense of nationhood, over centuries, even in a state of Diaspora, and they are inspired by an Afrikan Messiah, who preached liberation. In all of this they are empowered to name their reality and to claim their giftedness, both past and present, as they envision and embrace an emergent Africentric spirituality.

Stewart describes four building blocks that make up such a spirituality and result in what he calls "relational freedom."[11] The first is contiguity, which is a closeness that is at once physical, spiritual, and relational and provides "communal solidarity and strength in defiance of forces of disintegration and dissolution."[12] Second is imminence, which points to God's enduring presence and transformative power in time and space as an immediate intercession "on behalf of the black community."[13] The third is catharsis, which is the process of releasing anxieties and other barriers that inhibit freedom and is "an important part of individual and collective healing."[14] Finally, there is intimacy which provides the kind of staying power that "enables individuals to sustain vital bonds"[15] that fulfill their personhood and humanity.

I believe that contiguity and catharsis describe the impact of FAPC's reappropriation of time and ritual while imminence and intimacy capture their passionate embrace of their connection with a black Messiah. During each of the renamed liturgical periods, for example, this congregation taps into a collective power that emerges as they identify community in broader terms that include the Diaspora. Afrikan Consciousness,

Afrikan and Caribbean Liberation, and even the ancestors name additional dimensions of their lives together that give them physical, spiritual, and relational meaning. This connects them to an experience of the gospel that is more relevant to who they understand themselves to be. This level of contiguity, in turn, causes a catharsis that helps them to transcend the anxiety and fragmentation of their experience and prepares them to identify and live into their individual and collective giftedness. Mother's Day and Father's Day then cease to celebrate individual roles and embrace instead the black family in all its forms and configurations as the church moves from surviving to thriving.

Their identification with and belief in an Afrikan Messiah speaks to a level of imminence that gives reassurance and power. It affirms the abiding presence of a God who is acquainted with the vicissitudes of black life because God chose to don the robe of black flesh. But this is much more than a presence. It is acknowledgment of divine power that is able to act immediately on behalf of black people. Finally, through the assured presence of an Afrikan Messiah, FAPC experiences an immediate intimacy with God that heals and nurtures in ways that repair shattered bonds of kinship.[16] But it also helps to sustain and liberate relationships among the people, giving a level of autonomy that boldly speaks on behalf of its African sisters and brothers and all of God's people.

I believe that herein lies a significant example of the presence of Self-Determination and Cooperative Economics that is undergirded by Faith. This congregation boldly redefines time in a way that speaks more relevantly to their African American context and it is better equipped to cooperatively engage in the creation of its future. Through the redefined church calendar, this congregation solidifies its sense of individual and communal identity through Cooperative Economics and prepares itself for cooperative use of its gifts in the community. Through an unashamed embrace of an Afrikan Messiah, FAPC claims a sense of Self-Determination that has a divine locus that not only opens up wider avenues of power but also requires deeper levels of accountability. Together these principles are seen as the emergent contours of an Africentric spirituality that will help this congregation survive as well as thrive.

The members of this congregation have no naïve notion of the challenges that await them as they make radical claims about the union be-

tween their African and Christian identities in an increasingly individualistic and dichotomizing society. Their notion of Cooperative
Economics honors communality and cultivates human, spiritual, and intellectual capital, in addition to the more obvious connections to monetary and property resources. It also identifies and utilizes the gifts and talents of the church as well as the community as it seeks a holistic quality
of life for all. Likewise, expressions of Self-Determination are grounded
in an understanding of identity as an expression of the *imago dei* (image
of God) and celebrate an Afrikan Messiah. But unless these African-
centered principles are partnered with a strong Christ-rooted theology,
they lose their prophetic edge, making Cooperative Economics just another social service endeavor and reducing Self-Determination to affirmations of self-esteem that border on idolatry. Although not perfect,
FAPC has made and continues to make admirable efforts toward naming
and celebrating their giftedness as an African people in Diaspora as well
as claiming and accepting the responsibilities of sharing a gospel of empowerment and liberation. This brings together faith and culture in ways
that affirm and empower. In this we see the contours of an Africentric
spirituality that helps them to keep the faith in a congregational context.

TRINITY UCC

In forty-one years, Trinity has grown numerically as well as spiritually
in ways that would have been unimaginable to its founders. Its story revealed a goal of keeping the faith through commitments that took different forms. Through a journey from a "white church in black face,"
to a "black church in the black community," this congregation deepened and broadened its self-concept when seen through the lenses of
Unity and Purpose. These two principles functioned as two sides of the
same coin, revealing Unity as the basis of their relationship with God
and others and Purpose as their sacred vocation of service to God and
others. Together, they point to a communal consciousness grounded in
Faith that sustained them as Africans living in Diaspora.

Both of these principles, in their expanded forms, point to a theology of liberation. They express Jesus' proclamation to public ministry in
Luke 4:18 that preaches the gospel to the poor, proclaims release of the
captives, and recovers sight to the blind—all in acknowledgment that
God's time is always the right time. The poor, the captives, and the

blind, through the lenses of Unity and Purpose, transcend the physical to include the mind and spirit. This results in a holistic link that is in keeping with the African concept of harmony. Consequently, Unity cannot be experienced and expressed exclusively in the context of a congregation, denomination, or race but must at some point reach out to embrace the kind of communality that includes them all. Purpose, in a similar manner, should begin with the individual group as it acknowledges its self worth and celebrates its gifts. This helps Trinity resist the cultural blindness of assimilation while being acutely aware of the perils of an overly self-absorbed culture. But it must also be in touch with and responsive to the cries for liberation from those without power. In both cases, Purpose and Unity provide a template for surviving the realities of a contemporary life of exile as well as thriving in a world created and sustained by a just and loving God.

Soon after Trinity made the commitment to adopt a communal consciousness that linked it more closely to a theology of liberation and an African identity, it became necessary to find ways to carry out the content of this new self-understanding. One of the ways this happened was through the annual rituals and celebrations. As mentioned earlier, Umoja Karamu and Kwanzaa were instrumental in reminding Trinity of its connection to their past as they moved toward their future. Umoja Karamu was particularly significant because it symbolized the Unity feast of solidarity of the black family that corresponded to the celebration of Thanksgiving. Celebrated on Thanksgiving morning, the ritual tells the story of West African peoples through narrative and song, describing five historic periods of the black family. Each period corresponds to a color and a food that is eaten during the service. As the years progressed, Trinity added more elaborate dancing, singing, and drumming to deepen the experience and expand their expression of an Afrocentric spirituality. Umoja Karamu is clearly a ritual that speaks of Unity between the past, present, and future as it also highlights the ongoing Purpose of celebrating and sustaining kinship and familial ties.

Kwanzaa, from its early years, was a celebration for the congregation as well as the community. Ministries were organized into groups around the seven principles and each evening one grouping was asked to share how their works of ministry were examples of the assigned principle. This was an excellent way to celebrate the work of ministry while challenging the membership to reflect on each principle as an important value that goes beyond speaking to doing. This has been a way to unite the congregation around its commitment of being "Unashamedly Black and Unapologetically Christian" and to understand that one of their ongoing purposes is to keep the two in a creative and complementing tension.

Dona Maramba Richards, in *Let the Circle Be Unbroken: The Implications of African Spirituality in the Diaspora,* among other things discusses the multidimensional nature of ritual drama in African society, where it is understood on "metaphysical, religious, communal and psychological levels simultaneously."[17] It is through ritual drama, she postulates, that Africans in Diaspora found meaning in the midst of chaos and were able to resurrect life out of a communal experience of death.[18] As an "ultimate philosophical expression of the African worldview," these sacred rituals express Unity "as new life is given to the African spirit."[19] During slavery, the sacred repetition of rituals kept Africans sane in the midst of insanity and gave them courage to endure. It was psychologically healthy in that it provided a "communally constructive release of tension," that if left unattended could lead to socially destructive behavior and/or permanent psychological damage.[20] There is no doubt about the effectiveness of ritual drama in the lives of countless Africans in Diaspora as they sought ways to find meaning and to survive in a state of exile. Through ritual acts, they remembered their connection to the past but they were also re-membered and reconnected at a deeper spiritual level that opened the way for healing.

Richards goes on to say that ritual drama is cathartic and that catharsis is necessary for renewal. It is here that we see a cultural and spiritual Unity that moves toward a Purpose that is not simply to survive but to thrive. Ritual drama, particularly in the form of spirited worship, for example, feels good! It departs from the notion of human sacrality and relationality with God and it is manifested within community. It helps people effectively adapt, transform, and transcend their present reality and creates coping skills for survival and connects with Stewart's notion of creative soul force. But to remain here is to simply survive. It ignores the potential power to extend this ritual energy into a transforming and even transgressing presence that confronts the powers and principalities that reinforce human devaluation and oppression. The ritual drama can, if allowed, move persons from a surviving to thriving mode.

At Trinity, rituals like Umoja Karamu, Kwanzaa, and more recently the MAAFA[21] are clear expressions of Unity. They reestablish Trinity's relationship with God and others through a stronger sense of being and through Purpose as this congregation reclarifies its communal commitment to continue in its sacred vocation to serve their God and others. Keeping the Faith through the experience of ritual drama is an important way that this congregation affirms and celebrates the principles of Unity and Purpose when these principles are understood as a way to combine faith and culture. They also open the way for the emergence of an Africentric spirituality that is rooted in a theology of liberation and centered on realities of being Christians of African descent in exile in America.

Another important way that Unity and Purpose are seen at Trinity is in the way they "do" theology through activism. An earlier example of this included their partnership with others in the UCC in support of the release of the Wilmington Ten through letter writing and petition signings campaigns. But a key example of this activism on a more global level appeared in the early 1980s when they were only one of a few black congregations in Chicago that consented to place a "Free South Africa" sign on their lawn. While the display of a sign may seem like a small thing, it spoke volumes to those who passed by. It placed Trinity in a position to be questioned, criticized, and misunderstood by those who did not understand their prophetic vision of liberation, especially for black Africans across the Atlantic. This was evidence of an activism grounded in a prophetic call to join their sisters and brothers in the fight against apartheid in South Africa.

The prophetic function of the black church, says Peter Paris in his book *The Social Teaching of the Black Church,* was to utilize, "all available means to effect religious and moral reform in the society at large."[22] This function became necessary historically in an environment of racial segregation as African Americans had to do whatever they could to find some form of autonomy and dignity in a society that denied their basic humanity. Since Trinity decided that one of the ways that its commitment to religious and moral reform would be lived out was through social activism, their efforts to support black South Africans in their plight for liberation was not an unusual response. It was an act of Unity with others whose pain was felt on an intimate level and a call to the Purpose for liberation. Each was supported by an enduring Faith in a God of justice, mercy, and love.

In his book *We Have Been Believers: An African-American Systematic Theology,* James H. Evans Jr. posits that liberation was central to the African American church and its self-understanding from its inception,[23] and in many instances it became the catalyst for actions of resistance. Evans goes on to say, however, that this liberation is "not just the missiological thrust of the church, it is the essence of the church's identity. Liberation is not just what the church does; it is what the church is." This liberation finds its most meaningful expression in its dual existence within the "self-in-community," where the "self has no being apart from the community and the community is an abstraction apart from the collections of selves."[24] In this sense, a commitment to activism on behalf of black South Africans by Trinity is a bold statement that it is not simply aware of their plight but convinced of the presence of evil and convicted to help eradicate it for the sake of all. This speaks of a sense of Unity that is communal in nature supported by a Purpose that is prophetic in its thrust. The seriousness of this commitment was seen as this congregation used the Karios Document as a churchwide study in an effort to raise consciousness. This, in addition to earlier encounters with persons from South Africa in their midst, opened the way for them to truly identify on an intimate level and to be more diligent about finding ways to keep the Faith in a congregational context.

CONCLUSION

As we consider the direction of these congregations, it becomes clear that they are each a tremendous source of self-determination and pride and will contribute to the health and wholeness of the black community and the world in the twenty-first century. They are equipped with material and human resources that provide opportunities to address some of the more pressing issues of the day. They also encourage and nurture a level of spirituality that recaptures and taps into the wisdom of the past and reinterprets it for the future. But despite these very positive ways these congregations are able to provide avenues for hope and wholeness, there are a number of issues that can cause them to stray from the very commitments they profess, in the process of adapting and incorporating an Africentric perspective. These issues and trends relate directly back to the two common concepts they each try to embrace: maintaining harmony between the faith and culture and embracing communal values.

Maintaining harmony between the sacred and secular clearly provides an important balance for Africentric congregations, but when the voice of the secular is allowed to dominate, for example, a congregation becomes more cultural in its agenda. Then they run the risk of losing their prophetic voice, vision, and mission and move dangerously close to worshipping the culture rather than the Christ. On the other hand, when the sacred alone takes center stage, ritual and worship become the ultimate goal and are allowed to overshadow vital commitments to social justice. Africentric congregations cannot afford to slip into secular rhetoric that speaks against injustice and social ills without acknowledging the power of the gospel. Similarly they must guard against focusing solely on sacred responses of praise and adoration for their personal deliverance that ignore the suffering of others in the world. This kind of dichotomy is contrary to an African worldview that seeks to mirror the harmony and wholeness of God's creation. What is more beneficial is a commitment to the same sacred/secular blending that sustained and empowered their forebears. African-centered congregations must realize that power is still available to them to provide a sense of meaning that supports and directs them as they try to live their Faith in the midst of a complex and often unethical world.

Continuing the conversation, the support of communal values speaks volumes against the rampant trend toward individualism in this society. To embrace the African dictum, "I am because we are; we are, therefore, I am," emphasizes a communal value system that is not simply grounded in the exclusion of others but identifies both accountability and responsibility across family, kinship, and extended family relationships. To allow it to function exclusively within the immediate congregation, however, creates an atmosphere of exclusion that rejects people outside of that context. An even more insidious manifestation of this kind of closed communalism is the exclusion that occurs within the congregation itself, based on class, gender, age, and sexual orientation. A closed communalism is antithetical to the African worldview because it denies the sacredness of all of God's creation and ultimately the very sovereignty of God. The alternative is an open communalism that begins in the congregation and provides a strong sense of self-consciousness and a strong sense of God-consciousness that inform and require committed engagement in the community as well as the world.

I believe this research has highlighted both the promise and problems of these Africentric congregations in their attempt to maintain a balance between faith and culture as they walk the talk and keep the faith. Through their worship and ministries they show an undeniable goal of cultural and theological commitment. Each is aware of the challenges it faces and does not deny the possible pitfalls that can distort purpose or halt progress. While different in many ways, they all share a self-love that is inspired by the liberating gospel, which they are mandated to acknowledge, adhere to, and proclaim. I sincerely believe that these congregations provide examples for other churches, regardless of racial/ethnic makeup, because they are grounded in a love of God and a commitment to the sincere work of ministry in God's world. I also contend that if churches want to be on the cutting edge of society in the twenty-first century they must not separate their congregational identities into sacred and secular entities because it depletes their potential power for transformative ministry. In the same frame, they must not restrict their vision of ministry to their own backyard because it compromises the mandate of the gospel.

Any dedicated arborist knows that a tree is only as strong as its roots are deep. Although underground, the roots are an important part of the tree as they spread out in a diameter that measures one to two times the height of the tree, giving it a strong anchor as it seeks and provides water and oxygen. The health of the foliage and fruit consequently is dependent on a strong and sturdy root system. In addition to healthy roots, proper care of the branches through pruning is an important part of tree health. While improper pruning damages and delays growth, skillful cutting improves the health of the tree and promotes the production of fruit.

As three sturdy trees, Imani Temple Christian Fellowship, First Afrikan Presbyterian Church, and Trinity United Church of Christ claim the strong, solid roots of Christ as their primary nourishment and support. They understand that their Christian roots go back to the birth of Christian faith and are well established in the soil of Africa, watered by the matriarchs and patriarchs of old. They realize that Christianity did not emerge in a vacuum and that its dynamism is due to the richness of the cultural soil in which it was planted. These congregations also know that their section of the tree has blossomed despite principalities and powers designed to stunt their growth and abort their efforts to survive as well as thrive. Consequently, they understand the value of pruning branches to produce healthy fruit. Through their respective efforts to retell the Christian story of Africans in Diaspora, they cut away the branches of miseducation and self-hatred that narrow vision and stifle potential growth. Through this difficult and often painful pruning they made way for blossoms of self-love, partnering faith and culture in ways that strengthened their congregational walk and emboldened their congregational talk. In the stories of these three Africentric congregations we find the fruit of Unity, Self-Determination, Collective Work and Responsibility, Cooperative Economics, Purpose, and Creativity nourished by the roots of Faith. With this foundation they embrace a Christ-rooted, African-centered worldview that seeks a creative balance between faith and culture as they acknowledge a both/and approach to mission and ministry. Through these efforts they create the contours of an Africentric spirituality that empowers them to walk the talk and keep the faith as the sun-kissed daughters and sons of Africa who name and claim their Christian faith in America.

six

An Africentric Spirituality
in Everyday Use

IN A SHORT STORY, "Everyday Use," Alice Walker tells about a mother and her two daughters, Dee and Maggie, who were born and raised in the rural South. As the story unfolds, Dee returns home for a visit after moving away to college. During her time of study, she discovered the beauty and richness of her African heritage and, consequently, changed her name to Wangero Lee Wanika Kemayo to celebrate her new identity. Because of her heightened cultural awareness, she began to covet some of the items from home that once had no value for her. The reason for this trip was to collect two quilts that were handmade by her mother and grandmother that she wanted to display in her apartment. When she discovered that her mother promised them to her sister as a gift for her upcoming wedding, she said, "Maggie can't appreciate these quilts! She'll probably be backward enough to put them to everyday use." "I hope she will!" replied the mother.[1] Wangero saw the quilts as a visual statement of her heritage that celebrated her budding black consciousness and she wanted them as a reminder of her rich past. She looked to them as a reminder of an empowering reality beyond ordinary life, much like the purpose religious icons serve. Her intention was not to worship them but to allow their mystical presence to inform her identity.

In my own experience of becoming conscientious as a young adult, I was encouraged to learn more about my African heritage in my congregation. This new knowledge caused me to proudly wear African garb, to begin to appreciate people, places, and things associated with Africa, and to rethink my world and experiences from an African perspective. In each case, I was affirmed as I learned about my rich heritage. In the process, I gradually reversed negative images and definitions that kept me bound in a world of self-loathing. I replaced them with others that helped me love myself as God created me. At this early stage of black consciousness, I welcomed my new knowledge of Africa as it informed my identity, much like Wangero, but I was still not able to let it totally shape my actions. I could not yet put it into everyday use. I needed a way to actualize the energies from my emerging identity.

Many contemporary black congregations that self-identify as African-centered have a similar experience as they embrace and celebrate their African heritage. They engage in intentional study about their past and learn to appreciate people, places, and things that reflect their newfound knowledge. They adorn their sanctuaries and themselves in the fabric of the continent as they participate in the spirit-filled worship of the black religious experience. They acknowledge the black presence in the Bible, rethink the gospel message as one of liberation as well as salvation, and affirm a love for themselves as the sun-kissed children of mother Africa. But knowing how to translate these new convictions and perspectives into everyday use in the community and the world is not always easy. Congregations that want to take this next step must be committed to walking the talk and keeping the faith in both word and deed. In their efforts to integrate faith and culture, they must engage a broadened context that will open them up to more complex relationships. They will then find themselves asking different questions, identifying different issues, and conversing with different groups of people as they place faith and culture in conversation, allowing each to be informed, critiqued, and empowered by the other.

CONGREGATIONAL REFLECTION AND DISCUSSION

The following set of questions and exercises are designed to support pastors and lay leaders as they think seriously about the value of engaging in ministry from an Africentric perspective. The principles of Unity, Self-Determination, Collective Work and Responsibility, Cooperative Economics, Purpose, and Creativity are partnered with supporting scriptures that connect them more clearly to the undergirding principle of Faith. Returning to the restated definitions, exercises are suggested that begin to embrace an Africentric spirituality through a more informed awareness of the Diaspora. Together they will challenge leaders to think and respond on two levels—as a part of an individual congregation and as a part of the African Diaspora—as they deepen and broaden aspects of African culture in the context of Christian faith. During these learning experiences, leaders are encouraged to prayerfully explore and discern how these questions and exercises will best support their congregation where it is now and where it wants to go in the future. This should be done with the assurance that God speaks to congregations from within their own denominational, geographical, historical, and generational contexts and desires to move them toward fulfilling God's plan and purpose in their particular part of the vineyard.

Unity

Read and think a moment about Galatians 3:28: "There is no longer Jew or Greek, there is no longer slave or free, there is no longer male and female; for all of you are one in Christ Jesus." Keep in mind that the churches in the province of Galatia were made up of converted Jews and Gentiles. One of the major challenges of these churches came from the expectations of the Judaizers. These Jewish Christians insisted that Gentile converts become Jewish, through the rite of circumcision and the practice of dietary laws, as a prerequisite to becoming Christian. While Paul acknowledged the presence of the Mosaic law in the history of Israel, he gave a new message that faith in Christ provides freedom from sin in a way that the Law could not do. He revealed the good news that regardless of their former beliefs and practices, Jews and Gentiles alike were justified by faith alone and not by their works. Because of the love of God demonstrated through the sacrifice of Christ, there is a new experience of Unity that is inclusive and welcomes all as a part of the body of Christ. This

Unity in Christ eliminates barriers of exclusion but does not presuppose uniformity. It celebrates individual giftedness within the body of Christ.

Think about how your congregation includes as well as excludes others and discuss ways that there can be greater Unity.

- Consider the categories of Jew/Greek as different generations or lifestyles in your congregation, slave/free as different class or economic groups in your congregation and male/female as different gender relationships in your congregation and identify specific individuals and groups that fit these categories.
- Explore some of the ways that they are intentionally or unintentionally excluded or marginalized in your ministries.
- Create and discuss role-plays for each that illustrate when this happens in the life of your congregation and how people feel and respond when they are excluded.
- Discuss and create an outline for a ritual of inclusion to be used with each of these categories in your congregation in an effort to encourage greater Unity.

Now consider the expanded description of Unity as an expression of an African notion of communality that seeks a heightened Diaspora-consciousness made relevant in an American religious context: *To seek and maintain Unity that begins with our relationship with God, affirms our connection to Africa and the Diaspora, and calls forth solidarity among and liberation for all of God's people.*

- Think about and discuss ways that your congregation can use Bible study centered on the Jewish experience of exile to open the way for deeper understanding about what it means to be an African in the Diaspora.
- Find persons in your congregation and community who were born in various parts of the African Diaspora. Invite them to share their own personal experience and to assist your congregation as it explores the historical, geographical, political, and cultural background of their native homes.
- Discuss and create a plan for a series of churchwide studies (for adults, youth, children) on specific places in the Diaspora that will

create a greater awareness of your congregation's Unity and a stronger commitment to working with others for liberation.

Self-Determination

Read and think a moment about Genesis 1:27–28: "So God created humankind in his image, in the image of God he created them; male and female he created them. God blessed them, and God said to them, "Be fruitful and multiply, and fill the earth and subdue it." Consider the fact that the book of Genesis is the story of beginnings that describes creation that moved from chaos to order, from solitude to relationship, and from confusion to function. The cycles of nature were complemented by the presence of humankind, who received dominion and freedom as well as responsibility and accountability. The charge to multiply and subdue the earth should not be viewed as a disconnected autonomy but one that is linked, guided, and empowered by the Creator of the universe, who is the author of the world and the initiator of relationships. This autonomy has both a responsibility and accountability to self and others that carries with it the power to create, name, and sustain human reality. But when this charge failed to be grounded in and dependent on the divine presence, it resulted in separation and sin because of inappropriate expressions of self-determination.

- Think about the ways your congregation expresses Self-Determination and the challenges it faces maintaining a responsible and accountable autonomy.
- What are the various ways your congregation expresses its identity (race, congregation, denomination, community, etc.) and which one is most prominent?
- How does this identity translate into Self-Determination and what parts of your congregational reality are you able to create and name because of it?
- What are some of the examples of how your congregational autonomy to name and create have resulted in self-centered rather than community-centered ministry?
- How can your congregation claim an autonomy that is directed by God's divine mandate and responsive to the needs of the community?

- How can your congregation balance the celebration of itself with the concerns for others?

Now consider the expanded description of Self-Determination as an expression of an African notion of communality that seeks a heightened Diaspora consciousness made relevant in an American religious context: *To define ourselves as daughters and sons of Africa, created in the image of God, and willing to participate in the liberation of those in the Diaspora and the world.*

- Name and discuss the barriers and misconceptions about Africa that prevent many in your congregation from embracing their African identity.
- Invite members of the discussion group who are comfortable to share stories of when, where, and how they were first able to acknowledge and celebrate their African identity.
- Discuss ways that a more contextual study of the Bible can help create a broader Diaspora consciousness and cultivate a stronger commitment to supporting a theology of liberation.
- Explore ideas about how your congregation can encourage a positive self-identity among youth and children and support them as they learn to name and claim their own reality as Africans in Diaspora.

Collective Work/Responsibility

Read and think a moment about James 1:22–25. "But be doers of the word, and not merely hearers who deceive themselves. For if any are hearers of the word and not doers, they are like those who look at themselves in a mirror; for they look at themselves and, on going away, immediately forget what they were like. But those who look into the perfect law, the law of liberty, and persevere, being not hearers who forget but doers who act—they will be blessed in their doing." Keep in mind that this letter was written to "the twelve tribes in the Dispersion" (1:1) and it addressed some of the practical aspects of the Christian faith. It discussed taming the tongue, judging others, boasting, and patience in suffering as some of the challenges that Christians face in daily living. It emphasized faith as something that is alive, active, and manifested in works. This position is not, however, in contradiction to Paul's message that salvation comes through faith alone. It stresses, instead, that faith takes on its most transforming presence through actions; therefore, James states that faith without works is dead. He, like Paul, does not ignore the presence of the Law in the history of Israel and its importance in sustaining continuity for a people in Diaspora. Works for him become a manifestation of the "perfect Law" when they come as a result of action motivated by faith rather than obedience motivated by fear.

Consider your congregation's understanding of Collective Work/ Responsibility and think about it in terms of its relationship to faith and works—faith as a responsible way of being and works as collaborative efforts. Discuss the implications of these ideas for your congregation's ministry and mission.

- What are some of the experiences in your congregation when Collective Work/Responsibility is clearly seen?

- Think of ways that collective efforts in your congregation's ministries are more difficult? What do you think are the sources of these difficulties and how can they be addressed?

- Think about your congregation's ministry/mission as an experience of sacrament rather than an exercise of social work. Invite individual members in the discussion to give testimony about how they gained a greater sense of God's power and presence while helping others.

- Select two to three ministries and brainstorm ways that they can work in a more collective partnership with each other and provide more responsible service to others.

Now consider the expanded description of Collective Work/ Responsibility as an expression of an African notion of communality that seeks a heightened Diaspora consciousness made relevant in an American religious context: *To build and maintain our communities as Africans in Diaspora who live in a context of service and mutual accountability in America and the world, strengthened by the liberating spirit of God.*

- Examine the existing outreach experiences of your congregation with peoples in the Diaspora and discuss ways to make them more personal/relational. If none exist at the present, begin to discuss that possibility.

- Identify potential partners in your community (churches, agencies, schools) that can work together with you to strengthen your congregation's ties with the Diaspora.

- Take a look at your church's calendar and identify new times/events (other than Black History Month) when your congregation can celebrate the history and culture of specific countries/peoples in the Diaspora.

Cooperative Economics

Read and think a moment about Luke 12:48b: "From everyone to whom much has been given, much will be required; and from the one to whom much has been entrusted, even more will be demanded." This passage is located within a series of parables told by Jesus as he made his way toward Jerusalem and the crucifixion. After appointing and sending out the seventy, he continued his itinerant ministry of teaching, warning, encouraging, and admonishing through stories and sayings. This passage is the end of a discourse on the obligations of stewardship. He compares a faithful steward with one who is unfaithful and warns against sloth and indifference toward one's responsibilities as he reminds his audience that great blessings bring great responsibilities. As he "set his face toward Jerusalem," he provided the perfect example of the faithful steward that understood and accepted the great responsibilities of his charge.

Consider your congregation's understanding of Cooperative Economics as an obligation of individuals to exercise stewardship of time, talents, and treasures.

- Of the three (time, talents, treasures), where does your congregation place the most emphasis? Why?
- How do you think that a primary focus on only one of these areas limits the potential for individual members to be faithful stewards?
- How does this limitation affect the work of the ministries?
- List ideas about how your congregation can encourage a more balanced use of time, talents, and treasures within the membership and explore ways to make this a more faithful witness to God in the community.

Now consider the expanded description of Cooperative Economics as an expression of an African notion of communality that seeks a heightened Diaspora-consciousness that is made relevant in an American religious context: *To believe in and demonstrate a historic, multidimensional stewardship that values all resources, including material, human, intellectual, and spiritual, as gifts to us from God to be developed and used in African American communities, Diaspora, and the world for the good of all people.*

- Think about human resources as the available "people power" in your congregation, intellectual capital as the educational opportunities available in your congregation, spiritual capital as the ways you support and encourage faith formation within your congregation, and material capital as the physical property you possess as a congregation.

- Assign four groups that each explore the potential ways that one of these resources can more clearly reflect a commitment to the Diaspora.

- Plan a mission project for your congregation that further develops these material, intellectual, spiritual, and human resources. Include seminars/workshops that prepare persons for this experience.

Purpose

Read and think a moment about Micah 6:8: "He has told you, O mortal, what is good; and what does the Lord require of you but to do justice, and to love kindness, and to walk humbly with your God?" This prophet preached to Judah and Israel during the same time as Hosea and Isaiah. This was a time when the Jews had lost their original love for and devotion to the God of Abraham, Isaac, and Jacob. But unlike his contemporaries who framed their message around the political corruption of Jerusalem, Micah's prophesies emerged out of the context of a declining moral and religious life in the rural coastlands. His message was clearly one of doom but it also promised hope for those who would repent. This meant turning away from the idols and foreign gods that had seduced them while in Diaspora and returning their faith and allegiance to the God of their forebears. In this passage, Micah begins with a statement of moral fact—God has already told you what is good! But he goes on to ask a rhetorical question that speaks of three requirements: do justice, love kindness, and walk humbly with God.

Consider ways that your congregation should reflect on these requirements in light of its Purpose by focusing on its mission statement.

+ Read the congregational mission statement and discuss how it describes the overall Purpose of your ministries.
+ Are the issues of justice and kindness clearly stated? If so, identify the ways that this has been done. If not, think about how this statement can be rewritten in ways that will renew its Purpose in the direction of justice and kindness.
+ Discuss what it means for a congregation to walk humbly with God. How do you think that this relationship of humility with God can impact efforts toward justice and kindness in the church and community?

Now consider the expanded description of Purpose as an expression of an African notion of communality that seeks a heightened Diaspora consciousness made relevant in an American religious context: *To build and develop our communities in ways that acknowledge the sacredness of our collective work of liberation in the Diaspora and the world and our dependence on God's power and grace to perform it.*

+ How has your congregational Purpose opened the way for a broader commitment to the issues of the Diaspora?
+ Identify current issues of justice that your congregation already addresses or wishes to address and discuss how they are shaped by your faith commitment.
+ Include in your bulletin, on a regular basis, information about these issues that keeps your congregation in touch with their continuing impact on a particular part of the Diaspora.
+ Brainstorm various ways that this information can be highlighted through the life of your ministries (including youth/children) and how the leadership can encourage and support active responses.

Creativity

Read and think a moment about Isaiah 58:12: "Your ancient ruins shall be rebuilt; you shall raise up the foundations of many generations; you shall be called the repairer of the breach, the restorer of the streets to live in." During the time of Isaiah, Solomon's kingdom had been divided into north and south. While his contemporary, Hosea, prophesied to Israel in the north, he spoke a word on behalf of God to the inhabitants of the south. His message was a blend of rebuke and promise as he predicted the Babylonian captivity but also gave a word of hope for those who remained faithful. This passage of scripture announces the deliverance of God's people and God's power to both create and restore. It also states the requirements of Israel as God's servant nation and gives assurance of God's continued power and guidance in the process.

Think about your congregation's understanding of Creativity and consider its ability to be an institution that both creates and restores. Explore what this means in the life of your congregation.

- What are some of the areas in your congregational life where restoration and revitalization are needed? Think about and list some of the barriers preventing these changes and how they can be addressed.

- What are some of the areas in your community where your congregation can become a "repairer of the breach?"

- What ministry resources do you already have in place for this task and what is still needed?

- What new levels of faith commitment are required, both individually and collectively, for such a change and how can they be supported and sustained?

Now consider the expanded description of Creativity as an expression of an African notion of communality that seeks a heightened Diaspora consciousness made relevant in an American religious context: *To ground our creative energy in a renewed and renewing relationship with God that restores our African American communities and creates new possibilities for commitment to the Diaspora and the world for the benefit of all people.*

- Research articles in newspapers, magazines, and other sources that discuss the experiences and challenges of a particular country in the Diaspora as it tries to restore itself after war, famine, colonization, or the like and create a new way of life for its people.

- Trace this information over an extended period of time and determine what historical, political, and cultural information your congregation needs to know and understand about the justice issues that arise.

- Discuss ways that your congregation can use your local Creativity to advocate for this nation as it struggles for true liberation.

SUMMARY

It is essential for African American congregations to rethink the Nguzo Saba and discover ways to put them into everyday use. As your congregations consider these six principles, guided by the seventh (Faith), note the contours of an Africentric spirituality that is practice-oriented and that suggests an exilic theology that gives assurance of a home in both the land and ancestry of Africa. Embrace the values that are rooted in the Christian gospel and centered on the challenges and promise of living the Christian faith as Africans in Diaspora. Finally, embody the principles as they focus on a notion of communality that is made relevant for an American religious context that bring together faith and culture as you walk the talk and keep the faith.

Notes

Preface

1. Alice Walker, *In Love and Trouble: Stories of Black Women* (San Diego: Harcourt Brace Jovanovich, 1973), 118.

Introduction

1. James F. Hopewell, *Congregation: Stories and Structures,* ed. Barbara G. Wheeler (Philadelphia: Fortress Press, 1987), 14.

2. C. Ellis Nelson, *Where Faith Begins* (Richmond, Va.: John Knox Press, 1967), 36.

3. Hopewell, *Congregation,* 5.

4. James P. Wind and James W. Lewis, eds., *American Congregations, Volume 2: New Perspectives in the Study of Congregations* (Chicago: University of Chicago Press, 1994), 3–4.

5. Ibid., 8–9.

6. Wade Clark Roof, "Religion and Narrative," *Review of Religious Research,* 34, no. 4 (September 1993), 298.

7. Ibid., 301.

8. Djoli predates the more familiar term *griot,* which has origins in the French language and came into use as a result of nineteenth-century French colonization in West Africa. See Linda Goss and Marian E. Barnes, eds., *Talk that Talk: An Anthology of African American Storytelling* (New York: Orchard Books, 1989).

9. Robert M. Franklin, "The Safest Place on Earth: The Culture of Black Congregations," *American Congregations, Volume 2: New Perspectives in the Study of Congregations,* ed. James P. Wind and James W. Lewis (Chicago: University of Chicago Press, 1994), 257.

10. J. Deotis Roberts, *Africentric Christianity: A Theological Appraisal for Ministry* (Valley Forge, Pa.: Judson Press, 2000), 37.

11. See Delores Williams, *Sisters in the Wilderness: The Challenge of Womanist God-Talk* (Maryknoll, N.Y.: Orbis Books, 1993), and Diana Hayes, *Hagar's Daughters: Womanist's Ways of Being in the World* (New York: Paulist Press, 1995).

12. Roberts, *Africentric Christianity*, 37.

13. Theophus H. Smith, "The Spirituality of Afro-American Traditions," in *Christian Spirituality: Post-Reformation and Modern,* ed. Louis Dupre, Don E. Saliers, and John Meyendorff (New York: Crossroads, 1989), 402.

14. Charles Shelby Rooks, "Toward the Promised Land: An Analysis of the Religious Experience of Black Americans," in *The Black Church* 2 (1973), 1–48.

15. Smith, "Spirituality," 403.

16. Throughout the book, I will use the terms Africentric and African-centered interchangeably.

17. Roberts, *Africentric Christianity*, 18. Here Roberts describes the experience of oppression for African Americans as "more like an exile than an exodus." He then outlines Pan-Africanism, Negritude, Harlem Renaissance, and the black nationalism and the civil rights movements as ideological moments that laid a historical context for and understanding of Africentricity.

18. Roberts, *Africentric Christianity*, 72.

19. See Ndugu T'Ofori-Atta, *ChristKwanzaa: An African American Church Liturgy,* (Clifton, N.Y.: Strugglers' Community Press, 1990).

20. Roberts, *Africentric Christianity*, 77.

21. Maisha Sullivan, "The Nguzo Saba: African-Centered Values as Tools for Family Assessment, Support, and Empowerment," *National Parent Information Network, Virtual Library,* http://npin.org/library/2001/n00601/n00601.html. See also Gwynelle, *Practicing Kwanzaa Year Round: Affirmations and Activities Around the Seven Principles* (Summertown, Tenn.: Global Cultures, 2000); Janette Elizabeth Chandler Kotey, "A Program to Raise the Faith Level in African-American Children Through Scripture, Kwanzaa Principles and Culture," doctoral dissertation (World Cat), 1999; and Christopher L. Bishop, "Nguzo Saba: An Africentric Approach to Examining Self-Esteem, Africentrism and Behavior Modification with African-American Adolescents," doctoral dissertation (World Cat), 2002.

22. Mary Lefkowitz, *Not Out of Africa: How Afrocentrism Became an Excuse to Teach Myth as History* (New York: Basic Books, 1996). See also Cheryl Sanders, ed., *Living the Intersection: Womanism and Afrocentrism in Theology* (Minneapolis: Augsburg Fortress, 1995).

23. Iva. E. Carruthers, "For Such a Time as This: A Pan African Theopraxis," master's thesis, Garrett Evangelical Theological Seminary, 2000, 1–2.

24. C. Eric Lincoln, *The Black Church Since Frazier* (New York: Schocken Books, 1974).

25. See Molefe Asante, *Afrocentricity: The Theory of Social Change* (Buffalo, N.Y.: Amulefi Publishing, 1980), and *Kemet, Afrocentricity and Knowledge* (Trenton, N.J.: Africa World Press, 1990).

26. Molefe Asante, *The Afrocentric Idea* (Philadelphia: Temple University Press, 1987), 6.

27. Stephanie Aisha Steplight Johnson, "Molefi K. Asante's Afrocentric Paradigm: A Model for Multiculturalism," in *Molefi Kete Asante and Afrocentricity: In Praise and in Criticism,* ed. Dhyana Ziegler (Nashville: Winston Publishing, 1995), 233–34.

28. Steven Seidman, ed., *The Postmodern Turn: New Perspectives on Social Theory* (New York: Cambridge University Press, 1994,) 5.

29. See Katie G. Cannon, *Black Womanist Ethics* (Atlanta: Scholars Press, 1998); Jacquelyn Grant, *White Women's Christ and Black Woman's Jesus: Feminist Christology and Womanist Response* (Atlanta: Scholars Press, 1989); and Renita Weems, *Just a Sister Away: A Womanist Vision of Women's Relationships in the Bible* (Philadelphia: Innisfree Press, 1988).

30. Dwight N. Hopkins, *Introducing Black Theology of Liberation* (New York: Orbis Books, 1999), 156, 134.

31. Anthony B. Pinn, *The Black Church in the Post–Civil Rights Era* (New York: Orbis Books, 2002), 34.

32. Ibid., 26.

33. Cheryl Townsend Gilkes, "The Black Church as a Therapeutic Community: Areas of Suggested Research into the Black Religious Experience," *The Journal of the Interdenominational Theological Center* 8, 1 (1980): 29–44.

34. Cheryl Townsend Gilkes, "'Plenty Good Room . . .' in a Changing Black Church," in *One Nation Under God?: Religion and American Culture,* ed. Marjorie B. Garber and Rebecca L. Walkowitz (New York: Routledge, 1999), 171.

35. Ibid., 169.

Chapter 1

1. Cited by George Gallup Jr. and Timothy Jones in *The Next American Spirituality: Finding God in the 21st Century* (Colorado Springs: Victor/Cook Communications Ministries, 2000), 26.

2. George Gallup Jr., and D. Michael Lindsay, *Surveying the Religious Landscape: Trends in U.S. Beliefs* (Harrisburg: Morehouse Publishing, 1999), 1.

3. Jackson W. Carroll, *Mainline to the Future: Congregations for the 21st Century* (Louisville: Westminster John Knox Press, 2000), 24.

4. Robert Wuthnow, *After Heaven: Spirituality in America Since the 1950s* (Berkeley: University of California Press, 1998), 3.

5. Steve Jacobsen, *Heart to God, Hands to Work: Connecting Spirituality to Work* (Bethesda, Md.: Alban Institute, 1997), 11.

6. Wuthnow, *After Heaven,* 10.

7. Ibid., 3–5.

8. Ibid., 168.

9. Ibid., 196.

10. Ibid., 197.

11. Ibid., 192.

12. Michael I. N. Dash, Jonathan Jackson, and Stephen C. Rasor, *Hidden Wholeness, An African American Spirituality for Individuals and Communities* (Cleveland: United Church Press, 1997), 11.

13. Ibid., 25.

14. Ibid.

15. Ibid., 81.

16. Carlyle F. Stewart III, *Black Spirituality and Black Consciousness: Soul Force, Culture and Freedom in the African-American Experience* (Trenton, N.J.: Africa World Press, 1999), 71–72.

17. Robert M. Franklin, *Another Day's Journey: Black Churches Confronting the American Crisis* (Minneapolis: Fortress Press, 1997), 41–43.

18. Note that most of these practices are also found in congregations outside of the black religious tradition. For this discussion, however, they are identified as a part of the cultural experience at hand.

19. Maulana Karenga, *Kwanzaa: A Celebration of Family, Community and Culture* (Los Angeles: University of Sankore Press, 1997), 33–66.

20. Maulana Karenga, *Introduction to Black Studies,* 2nd ed. (Los Angeles: University of Sankore Press, 1993), 173.

21. Maulana Karenga and Jacob Carruthers, eds., *Kemet and the African Worldview: Research, Rescue and Restoration* (Los Angeles: University of Sankore Press, 1986), 85.

22. Karenga, *Introduction to Black Studies,* 173.

23. Ibid., 174.

24. Karenga, *Kwanzaa*, 64.

25. Ibid., 43.

26. Ibid., 43–48.

27. Ibid., 48.

28. Ibid., 48-51.

29. Ibid., 51.

30. Ibid., 51–54.

31. Ibid., 55.

32. Ibid., 57.

33. Ibid., 58.

34. Ibid., 58–60.

35 Ibid., 61.

36. This is the ethical framework of Kawaida that affirms truth, justice, and righteousness as the foundation of the "right order established at creation . . . in the context of the divine, natural and social." See Karenga, *Kwanzaa*, 35.

37. Karenga, *Kwanzaa*, 61–64.

38. Ibid., 64–65.

39. Forrest E. Harris Sr., James T. Roberson, and Larry George, eds., vol. 1, and Lewis V. Baldwin, ed., vol. 2, *What Does It Mean to Be Black and Christian: Pulpit, Pew and Academy in Dialogue,* (Nashville: Townsend Press, 1995, 1996).

40. Ibid., 143–44.

41. Ibid.

42. Dorothy Bass, ed., *Practicing Our Faith: A Way of Life for Searching People* (San Francisco: Jossey-Bass, 1997), 6.

Chapter 2

1. Mrs. Muriel Cloyd, interviewed by author, Pomona, California, October 14, 2002. Mrs. Cloyd, the mother of Pastor Jelani F. Kafala, provided her home as the worship space for Imani Temple for the first eleven months of its existence.

2. Monette Rayford, e-mail interview with author, November 7, 2002.

3. This name means, "mighty hope for the future, for whom one has died." Jelani F. Kafala interviewed by author, October 12, 2002.

4. Maulana Karenga, *Introduction to Black Studies,* 2nd ed. (Los Angeles: University of Sankore Press, 1993), 458.

5. Iris V. Cully and Kendig Brubaker Cully, eds., *Harper's Encyclopedia of Religious Education* (San Francisco: Harper & Row, 1990), 357–58.

6. ITCF statement, March 2001, 5.

7. Kathy Kafela, interviewed by author, October 17, 2002.

8. Milton C. Sernett, *Bound for the Promised Land: African American Religion and the Great Migration* (Durham, N.C.: Duke University Press, 1997), 3.

9. Ibid., 14. See also Jonathan Earles and Mark C. Carnes, series eds., *The Routledge Atlas of African American History* (New York: Routledge, 2000), 68.

10. Quintard Taylor, "In Search of African American History in the West," *Smithsonian National Museum of African American History,* Behring Center, http://americanhistory.si.edu/paac/aquest/qtaylor.htm.

11. Stuart A. Gabriel and Joe P. Pattey, "Leaving Los Angeles: Migration, Economic Opportunity and Quality-of-Life," Southern California Studies Center, University of Southern California. http://www.frbsf.org/econrsrch /workingp/wp96-10.pdf.

12. Public Policy Institute of California, news release, May 8, 2002, http://www.ppic.org/publications/CalCounts12/calcounts12.press.html.

13. ITCF Founder's Day statement, 2002.

14. ITCF statement, March 2001, 21.

15. Ibid., 5.

16. *Los Angeles Metropolitan Churches 2000/01 Annual Report,* 6.

17. Observation of a meeting on October 15, 2002.

18. *Los Angeles Metropolitan Churches 2000/01 Annual Report,* 20.

19. Ibid., 19.

20. Ibid., 24.

21. Ibid., 25.

22. Kennon Mitchell, phone interview by author, May 22, 2003.

23. Ibid.

24. Dr. Mitchell's doctoral research centered on this very issue and he collected data over a three-year period as he evaluated the program at Frisbee Middle School.

25. Mitchell said that women mentors were selected from his staff as well as from among other colleagues.

26. The fellowship ministries include Man4mation, Women Seeking Christ, Urbanation, Glory Phi God Society, Single No More, and Fit to Be Tied. They each engage in intentional Bible study that relates to the challenges and concerns of the group. There are other ministries that support worship: Da Lawd Praise Team, For Peace Music Ministry, and Tribe of Levi Sanctuary Leaders. Culture, Bible study, and life skills are enhanced in a variety of culturally focused educational activities: the Imani Village after-school,

Sunday children's church, and adult Masterlife Institute classes, and development of financial skills through Power Corporation.

27. While it may seem to be a contradiction to "appoint" members to the council and still claim an egalitarian model, Kafela explains that it was necessary for him to select this first class of elders because of the newness of the congregation. In the future, however, they will be chosen through a more democratic process.

28. ITCF statement, March 2001, 14.

29. Observation of Council of Elders meeting, October 14, 2002.

30. These riots yielded fifty-three deaths, ten thousand arrests, twenty-three thousand injuries, more than a thousand burned buildings, and an estimated one billion dollars in damages for the city. See Kimberly Hohman, *Race Relations Newsletter,* "LA Riots, Ten Years Later," http//f.about.com/z/js/spr085m.htm.

31. Ibid. Magic Johnson purchased several movie theaters, two Starbucks, and a T.G.I. Friday's restaurant in the Crenshaw community. Likewise, Keyshawn Johnson opened a shopping center and a Home Depot.

32. Erin Aubry Kaplan, "Ten Years and a Cloud of Dust: Crenshaw in Slow Motion," *LA Weekly,* April 26–May 2, 2002, http//www.laweekly.com/ink/102/03/the-kaplan.php.

33. Maulana Karenga, *Kwanzaa: A Celebration of Family, Community and Culture* (Los Angeles: University of Sankore Press, 1997), 61.

34. Ibid., 63.

35. Carlyle Fielding Stewart III, *Black Spirituality and Black Consciousness: Soul Force, Culture and Freedom in the African-American Experience* (Trenton, N.J.: Africa World Press, 1999), 2.

36. Jackson W. Carroll and Wade Clark Roof, *Bridging Divided Worlds: Generational Cultures in Congregations* (San Francisco: Jossey-Bass, 2002), 5.

37. Tom Beaudoin, *Virtual Faith: The Irreverent Spiritual Quest of Generation X* (San Francisco: Jossey-Bass, 1999), 28.

38. Carroll and Roof, *Bridging Divided Worlds,* 65. See also Richard Flory and Donald E. Miller, eds., *Gen X Religion* (New York: Routledge, 2000).

39. Carroll and Roof, *Bridging Divided Worlds,* 80.

40. Karenga, *Kwanzaa,* 51.

41. Ibid., 52.

42. Ibid., 53.

43. Jackson Carroll, *Mainline to the Future: Congregations for the 21st Century* (Louisville: Westminster John Knox Press, 2000), 51–52.

44. Carroll and Roof, *Bridging Divided Worlds,* 202.

Chapter 3

1. Adapted from the First Afrikan Presbyterian Church affirmation recited each Sunday.

2. This word has been used at FAPC since 1993 as an alternative way of saying "Amen," meaning "so it is," "it is so," "it is established." It is spelled Axe, but pronounced ah-sheh' and finds its roots in the culture of the Yoruban people, exiled to Brazil by the Portuguese. It is connected to the powers of Eshu in the Candomble religion of Brazil. Eshu is the "polymorphous master of axe, the spiritual life force, the mystical power of the Orishas." The use of this term, then, represents more than a surface affirmation. It acknowledges and intersects with the spiritual essence of a person, thing, or experience. See Abdias do Nascimento, *Africans in Brazil: A Pan African Perspective* (Trenton, N.J.: Africa World Press, 1992), 55, 181. See also Philip John Neimark, *The Way of the Orisha: Empowering Your Life through the Ancient African Religion of Ifa* (San Francisco: HarperCollins, 1993).

3. Written by Malvis Alexander, minister of music, and sung each week in the Sunday worship services.

4. Ricky Stapleton, phone interview by author, August 17, 2003.

5. Ernest Trice Thompson, *Presbyterians in the South, 1861–1890, Vol II* (Richmond, Va.: John Knox Press, 1973), 195–6.

6. Ibid., 202.

7. Movement into the Baptist church, whose polity placed a lower emphasis on an educated clergy, became attractive for many leaving the Presbyterian Church. Additionally, the newly forming African Methodist Episcopal Church and later the Africa Methodist Episcopal Zion and the Colored Methodist Episcopal churches also attracted many.

8. Thompson, *Presbyterians in the South,* 202.

9. Ibid., 315.

10. Gayraud S. Wilmore, "Identity and Integration: Black Presbyterians and Their Allies in the Twentieth Century," in Milton J. Coalter, John M. Mulder, and Louis B. Weeks, eds., *The Diversity of Discipleship: Presbyterianiam and the 20th Century Christian Witness* (Louisville: Westminster John Knox Press, 1991).

11. Franklin C. Talmage, (prepared by Virginia [Mrs. Ben C.] Morris), "History of the Salem Presbyterian Church, Lithonia, Georgia, DeKalb County, 1875–1953," 3, 5, unpublished record from archives, Local Church History Program, Georgia Box 5 (dissolved churches), Presbyterian Historical Society, Philadelphia, Pa.

12. Robert D. Bullard, ed., *Sprawl City: Race, Politics and Planning in Atlanta,* (Washington, D.C.: Island Press, 2000), 8.

13. Laura Durojaiye, interviewed by author, November 13, 2002.

14. Bullard, *Sprawl City,* 11. By the 1990s Metropolitan Atlanta had ten counties that included Cherokee, Cobb, Douglas, Clayton, Fayette, Fulton,

Henry, Gwinnett, Dekalb, and Rockdale. The majority of African Americans find residence in DeKalb, Fulton, Cobb, and Gwinnett, where middle-income families have chosen black neighborhoods over integrated or all white areas.

15. Mark A. Lomax, interviewed by author, November 19, 2002.

16. Ibid. He and his wife cofounded the Gospel Experience on the campus of Virginia Tech.

17. Lomax later solidified his thought in his doctoral dissertation, "The Effects of an Afrocentric Hermeneutic in a Developing Congregation," United Theological Seminary in Dayton, Ohio, 1995.

18. Otis C. Thomas, phone interview by author, October 23, 2004.

19. The city of Atlanta in the late twentieth century has been a place of extended economic opportunity for African Americans and this is reflected quite clearly in the activities of its black churches. One of the most influential teachings in recent years has come from a number of churches that teach a "prosperity gospel," which many members of FAPC cannot embrace. These churches focus on personal health and wealth and some have resulted in megachurches that count over twenty thousand members, such as New Birth Missionary Baptist Church, led by Bishop Eddie Long, and World Changers Church, International, led by Rev. Creflo Dollar. See Alton B. Pollard III, "The Civic Impact of the Black Church in Atlanta," in *The Status of Black Atlanta, 2002* (Atlanta: Southern Center for Studies in Public Policy, Clark Atlanta University, 2000).

20. The Ankh is the symbol of life in ancient Egyptian culture; the biblical passage from Psalm 68:31 speaks of Ethiopia stretching her hands to God; and the red, black, and green are the colors of the liberation flag, popularized by Marcus Garvey. Together they link the African past with a biblical passage that affirms liberation and self-determination for peoples of African descent in the spirit of Garvey and others.

21. Will Coleman, interviewed by author, November 21, 2002.

22. Inger Anderson, interviewed by author, November 20, 2002.

23. Grace Cheptu, interviewed by author, November 20, 2002.

24. Securing its charter only nine months after starting, FAPC was the earliest in the history of the Atlanta Metro Presbytery to do so.

25. Mark A. Lomax "Liturgical Calendar," *Talking Drums,* 1, no. 8 (October 2002), 2.

26. Freddie and Mary Young, interviewed by author, November 19, 2002.

27. *First Afrikan Presbyterian Church, New Member Handbook,* October 2002, 7.

28. Susan Mitchell, interviewed by author, November 18, 2002.

29. Mekeyah McQueen, phone interview by author, November 13, 2003.

30. Peter Paris, *The Spirituality of African Peoples: The Search for a Common Moral Discourse* (Minneapolis: Fortress Press, 1995), 68.

31. Gayraud S. Wilmore, *Black and Presbyterian: The Heritage and the Hope* (Louisville: Witherspoon Press, 1998), 66.

32. "Is This New Wine?" Paper presented by African American Presbyterians for Prayer, Study and Action, August 22, 1993, 8.

33. Deborah Jackson, interviewed by author, November 19, 2002.

34. Deborah Jackson, "The Need for a Community Agenda," *Talking Drums,* FAPC monthly newsletter, 1, no. 9 (November 2002), 3.

35. First Afrikan Community Development Corporation brochure, 2002.

36. Aminata Umoja, interviewed by author, November 19, 2002.

37. First Afrikan Community Development Corporation brochure, 2002.

38. Gene Stephenson, interviewed by author, November 19, 2002.

39. First Afrikan Community Development Corporation brochure, 2002.

40. Dr. Will Coleman, "Beresheit (In the Beginning): Genesis 1:1," *Talking Drums,* FAPC monthly newsletter, 1, no. 2 (February 2002), 5.

41. Teresa Snorton, interviewed by author, November 18, 2002.

42. *About FAPC,* "Our History," www.fapc.org.

43. Maulana Karenga, *Kwanzaa: A Celebration of Family, Community and Culture* (Los Angeles: University of Sankore Press, 1997), 50.

44. Kelly Brown Douglas, *The Black Christ* (Maryknoll, N.Y.: Orbis Books, 1999), 79. See also Albert Cleage, *Black Christian Nationalism: New Directions for the Black Church* (New York: William Morrow, 1972), xv.

45. Douglas, *The Black Christ,* 56.

46. Ibid., 58.

47. Carlyle Fielding Stewart III, *Black Spirituality and Black Consciousness: Soul Force, Culture and Freedom in the African-American Experience* (Trenton, N.J.: Africa World Press, 1999), 27.

48. Ibid.

Chapter 4

1. Romney Payne, interviewed by author, September 3, 2002.

2. This concern was expressed in most religious institutions of this time. One of the primary questions was whether or not the church as an organization should take a stand on controversial social issues. See Wade Clark Roof, *Community and Commitment: Religious Plausibility in a Liberal Protestant Church* (New York: Eiserier, 1978), 3.

3. The UBC was organized in 1970 by Dr. Charles E. Cobb, then the executive director of the Commission for Racial Justice of the United Church of Christ.

4. Working along with the Commission for Racial Justice (CRJ) and the Ministers for Racial and Social Justice (MRSJ) the energy and resources

of those in the caucus created a solid black core within the UCC that could begin to accomplish what civil rights and integration failed to do.

5. Patricia Eggleston, interviewed by author, September 16, 2002.

6. S. L. Allen, interviewed by author, September 18, 2002.

7. This geographic designation began during the 1920s and remained through the 1940s to describe the physical boundaries of the predominant African American neighborhood in Chicago. See Glen E. Holt and Dominic A. Pacyga, *Chicago: A Historical Guide to the Neighborhoods—The Loop and South Side* (Chicago: Chicago Historical Society, 1979).

8. Sydney E. Ahlstrom, *A Religious History of the American People* (New Haven: Yale University Press, 1972), 950–51.

9. Kenneth B. Smith, interviewed by author, Chicago, Illinois, February 6, 1996.

10. Rev. Dr. W. Sterling Cary, interviewed by author, Chicago, Illinois, June 5, 1996. Cary states that historically the Congregational Christian Church in Illinois made special efforts to seek out "high potential" churches within the black community. These were African American congregations and communities that were "most like" white churches and were more likely to assimilate into the form and function of the denomination, according to Cary. As the first African American conference minister in the UCC, he served from 1974 to 1994. He admitted very candidly that his major task as conference minister in Illinois was to "move away from an exclusively white agenda, to provide more inclusivity in the denomination, and to focus on the power of the gospel to hear what we don't want to hear." This included inequity of the "high potential" measure for black churches.

11. Years later, Smith worked with Faulkner at the Congregational Church of Park Manor.

12. These families came from Lincoln Memorial Congregational Church, the Church of the Good Shepherd, South Congregational Church, and the Congregational Church of Park Manor.

13. Rev. Dr. Jeremiah A. Wright Jr., interviewed by author, March 25, 1996. Wright stated that for many African Americans in northern cities, their sole purpose for joining a mainline Protestant church was to get away from the black religious experience.

14. Wright interview. See also Wade Clark Roof, "Race and Residence in American Cities," *The Annals of the American Academy of Political and Social Science*, vol. 441 (Jan. 1979), 6–7.

15. Dr. Smith went on to serve as minister of Urban Affairs for the Community Renewal Society (1966–1968); senior pastor of the Church of the Good Shepherd (1968–1984); president of Chicago Theological Seminary (1984–1999); member of the Chicago school board 1979–82 (president

1980–81); and member of the board of the Chicago Community Trust (1999–present).

16. Rev. Willie J. Jamerson, interviewed by author, June 18, 1996. Jamerson came to Trinity by way of Nashville, Tennessee, and Roanoke, Virginia. He became convicted to enter the ministry and the UCC through his experiences at LeMoyne-Owen University in Memphis, Tennessee. Later his two-year term as the pastor of Howard UCC was followed by a brief tenure as the community supervisor for the Total Action Against Poverty program (a part of President Johnson's War on Poverty plan) in Virginia.

17. Wilmore, *Black Religion and Black Radicalism: An Interpretation of the Religious History of African Americans* (New York: Orbis Books, 1998), 222. See also Vincent Harding, *Hope and History: Why We Must Share the Story of the Movement* (New York: Orbis Books, 1990).

18. Wright interview.

19. Barbara J. Allen, interviewed by author, March 3, 1996.

20. This term refers to the status of having a middle income as well as the tendency to adopt the middle-class values of the dominant culture that focus more on individual and less on communal achievements.

21. Mr. Vallmer E. Jordan, interviewed by author, March 12, 1996. He observed that during this period in Trinity's history, its members, along with other middle-class African Americans, were enjoying the benefits of integration and saw themselves as representing the possibilities of further black progress.

22. See Kathleen Cleaver and George Katsiaficas, eds., *Liberation, Imagination and the Black Panther Party: A New Look at the Panthers and Their Legacy* (New York: Routledge, 2000).

23. This Chicago-based program, led by Rev. Jesse L. Jackson Jr., was the economic arm of the Southern Christian Leadership Conference founded by Dr. Martin Luther King Jr. in 1957.

24. Reuben A. Sheares III was a staff person at the Community Renewal Society (CRS) when he accepted the part-time position of interim pastor at Trinity. After Wright was called, he returned to CRS but later went on to the position of CEO of the Office of Church Life and Leadership of the UCC. He later returned to Chicago and served as senior pastor of the Congregational Church of Park Manor until his death in 1992.

25. Written by Vallmer E. Jordan, 1971. See also "25th Year of Ministry," Trinity United Church of Christ, 1986.

26. A correspondence dated October 27, 1971, to Val Jordan, chairperson of the Search Committee, from Fred G. Traut, associate conference minister, included profiles of five candidates: Rev. John Mickle, Rev. Thomas Davis, Rev. Harold David Long, Rev. Winston E. Waugh, and Rev. Richard Jones.

27. W. E. B. DuBois, *The Souls of Black Folk* (New York: New American Library, 1969), 45.

28. Mr. Jeffrey P. Radford and the People's Unity Ensemble found refuge at Trinity when they were looking for a place to rehearse in the fall of 1972. Upon discovering Radford's musical talents, the church asked him to provide musical leadership for Trinity's Youth Fellowship Choir, which later became the Trinity Choral Ensemble. As the years progressed, he assisted with Trinity's Chancel Choir as well as assumed full direction of the Little Warriors for Christ. This was just the beginning of his growing ministry of music at Trinity that gave birth to the Sanctuary Choir, the Women's and Men's Choruses, and Imani Ya Watume. Before his untimely death in August 2002, Dr. Radford's genius was known locally as well as nationally and internationally as he touched hearts, inspired souls, and empowered spirits through his music.

29. Cora I. Allen-Brown, interviewed by author, April 15, 2003.

30. Rev. Melbalenia D. Evans, interviewed by author, March 16, 2004. Rev. Evans currently serves as the executive minister of Trinity UCC.

31. This was a national office of the UCC dedicated to the task of addressing racism and injustice within the church and the world and keeping the conscience of the UCC on the cutting edge relative to the integrity of its Christian witness and its sensitivity of the black agenda.

32. *Trinity Annual Report*, "Executive Council Report," 1976.

33. Others arrested included eight black boys and one white woman. Their combined sentences totaled 282 years. See Rev. Benjamin F. Chavis, "The Wilmington, N.C., Ten Case," in *An American Political Prisoner Appeals for Human Rights in the United States of America,* United Church of Christ Commission for Racial Justice, 1978, 6.

34. Wright interview. After nearly a decade of steady growth, the numbers increased even more after the congregation began weekly radio broadcasts in 1980. From that time on, Trinity never took in fewer than three hundred members in a given year.

35. See, Jini Kilgore, ed., *What Makes You So Strong? Sermons of Joy and Strength from Jeremiah A. Wright, Jr.,* (Valley Forge: Judson Press, 1993) and Good News: Sermons of Hope for Today's Families (Valley Forge, PA: Judson Press, 1995).

36. Kairos Theologians (Group), *The Kairos Document, Challenge to the Churches: A Theological Comment on the Political Crisis in South Africa,* (Grand Rapids, Mich.: W.B. Eerdman's, 1986).

37. Shirley Bims-Ellis, interviewed by author, June 8, 2004.

38. Frances D. Harris, interviewed by author, June 12, 2004.

39. Despite the availability of the *Manual for Black Perspectives in Church Education,* published by the Joint Educational Development project in the mid–1970s, few relevant resources were available to support the growing congregational commitment to combine faith and culture. Trinity developed its own curricular outlines that integrated the Christian story with the struggles for freedom and liberation of African American people. They later used a relevant but limited curricular series called "Faith Journey" for youth and children published by the UCC.

40. Aletta Jumper, interviewed by author, July 30, 2004.

41. Dr. Elkin T. Sithole taught anthropology and ethnomusicology at Northeastern Illinois University's Center for Inner City Studies. His special field included African culture and the music of Africa and social change.

42. Iva E. Carruthers, interviewed by author, April 18, 2002.

43. Iva E. Carruthers, "A Testimony to Gye Nyame (Only God)," in *The Trinity Trumpet,* 1, no. 4 (October 2002), 22.

44. St. Clair Drake and Horace R. Cayton, *Black Metropolis* (New York: Harcourt & Brace, 1945).

45. Na'im Akbar, *Know Thy Self* (Tallahassee, Fla.: Mind Productions and Associates, 1998), 20.

46. Ibid., 28.

47. Anthony E. Pinn, *The Black Church in the Post-Civil Rights Era,* (New York: Orbis Books, 2002), 18.

Chapter 5

1. Gayraud Wilmore, *Black Religion and Black Radicalism: An Interpretation of the Religious History of African Americans* (New York: Orbis Books, 1998), 7. See also Martin dePorres Walsh, O.P., Eusebius of Caesarea, Ecclesiastical History, II 1, 3, in *The Ancient Black Christians* (San Francisco: Julian Richardson, 1969); and *The Church of Ethiopia: A Panarama of History and Spiritual Life* (Addis Ababa, Ethiopia: Ethiopian Orthodox Church, 1970).

2. Peter Paris, *The Spirituality of African Peoples: The Search for a Common Moral Discourse,* (Minneapolis: Fortress Press, 1995), 129.

3. Ibid., 22.

4. Ibid., 130.

5. www.pcusa.org/101/101-whoare.htm.

6. The first Egyptian dynasty was founded at Memphis by King Menes in 3100 B.C.E. See Earl Walter Faruq, "The Power of Spiritual Determinism in Ancient Egyptian City Life," in *Kemet and the African Worldview, Research,*

Rescue and Restoration, ed. Maulana Karenga and Jacob Carruthers (Los Angeles: University of Sankora Press, 1986), 71, 73.

7. June 19, 1865, was the date when Union soldiers landed in Galveston, Texas, with the news of the end of the war and the freedom of the slaves. See www.juneteenth.com/history.htm.

8. Mark A. Lomax, *Talking Drums,* FAPC monthly newsletter, 1, no. 8 (October 2002), 3.

9. Albert Cleage, *Black Christian Nationalism: New Directions for the Black Church* (New York: William Morrow, 1972), 47–49.

10. Ibid., 45.

11. Carlyle Fielding Stewart III, *Black Spirituality and Black Consciousness: Soul Force, Culture and Freedom in the African American Experience* (Trenton N.J.: Africa World Press, 1999), 75.

12. Ibid., 78.

13. Ibid.

14. Ibid., 81.

15. Ibid., 76.

16. Ibid., 85.

17. Dona Maramba Richards, *Let the Circle Be Unbroken: The Implications of African Spirituality in the Diaspora* (Trenton, N.J.: Red Sea Press, 1989), 26. See also Victor Turner, *The Ritual Process* (New York: Cornell University Press, 1969).

18. Richards, *Let the Circle Be Unbroken,* 23–24.

19. Ibid.

20. Ibid., 27.

21. This Swahali term, meaning "great suffering," refers to the holocaust of the Middle Passage and slavery in the Pan African experience. See Erriel Kofi Addae *The Maafa and Beyond* (Columbia Md.: Kugichagulia Press, 1995). See also Marimba Ani, *Yuguru: An African-centered Critique of European Cultural Thought and Behavior* (Trenton, N.J.: Africa World Press, 1994).

22. Peter J. Paris, *The Social Teachings of the Black Church* (Philadelphia: Fortress Press, 1988), 11.

23. James H. Evans Jr., *We Have Been Believers: An African-American Systematic Theology* (Minneapolis: Fortress Press, 1992), 135.

24. Ibid.

Chapter 6

1. Alice Walker, *In Love and Trouble: Stories of Black Women* (San Diego: Harcourt Brace, 1973), 57.

Selected Bibliography

Addae, Erriel Kofi. See Roberson, Erriel D.

Ahlstrom, Sydney E. *A Religious History of the American People.* New Haven, Ct.: Yale University Press, 1972.

Akbar, Na'im. *Know Thy Self.* Tallahassee, Fla.: Mind Productions and Associates, 1998.

Ani, Marimba. *Yurugu: An African-centered Critique of European Cultural Thought and Behavior.* Trenton N.J.: Africa World Press, Inc., 1994.

Asante, Molefe. *Afrocentricity: The Theory of Social Change.* Buffalo: Amulefi Publishing, 1980.

Bass, Dorothy, ed. *Practicing Our Faith: A Way of Life for Searching People.* San Francisco: Jossey-Bass, 1997.

Beaudoin, Tom. *Virtual Faith: The Irreverent Spiritual Quest of Generation X.* San Francisco: Jossey-Bass, 1999.

Bishop, Christopher L. *Nguzo Saba: An Africentric Approach to Examining Self-Esteem, Africentrism and Behavior Modification with African-American Adolescents.* Doctoral dissertation (World Cat), 2002.

Bullard, Robert D., ed. *Sprawl City, Race, Politics and Planning in Atlanta.* Washington, D.C.: Island Press, 2000.

Cannon, Katie G. *Black Womanist Ethics.* Atlanta: Scholars Press, 1998.

Carroll, Jackson W. *Mainline to the Future: Congregations for the 21st Century.* Louisville: Westminster John Knox Press, 2000.

Carroll, Jackson W., and Wade Clark Roof. *Bridging Divided Worlds: Generational Cultures in Congregations.* San Francisco: Jossey-Bass, 2002.

Carruthers, Iva E. *For Such a Time as This: A Pan African Theopraxis.* Master's thesis, Garrett Evangelical Theological Seminary, 2000.

_____. "A Testimony to Gye Nyame (Only God)." *In The Trinity Trumpet.* 1, no. 4 (October, 2000). 22

Cleage, Albert. *Black Christian Nationalism:New Directions for the Black Church.* New York: William Morrow, 1972.

Cleaver, Kathleen, and George Katsiaficas, eds. *Liberation, Imagination and the Black Panther Party:A New Look at the Panthers and Their Legacy.* New York: Routledge, 2000.

Cully, Iris V., and Kendig Brubaker Cully, eds. *Harper's Encyclopedia of Religious Education.* San Francisco: Harper & Row, 1990.

Dash, Michael, I. N., Jonathan Jackson, and Stephen C. Rasor. *Hidden Wholeness: An African American Spirituality for Individuals and Communities.* Cleveland: United Church Press, 1997.

Douglas, Kelly Brown. *The Black Christ.* Maryknoll, N.Y.: Orbis Books, 1999.

Drake, St Clair and Horace R. Cayton. *Black Metropolis.* New York: Harcourt & Brace, 1945.

DuBois, W. E. B. *The Souls of Black Folk.* New York: American Library, 1969.

Dupre, Louis, Don E. Saliers, and John Meyendorff, eds. *Christian Spirituality: Post-Reformation and Modernity.* New York: Crossroad, 1989.

Earles, Jonathan, and Mark C. Carnes, eds. *The Routledge Atlas of African American History.* New York: Routledge, 2000.

Evans, James H. Jr. *We Have Been Believers: An African-American Systematic Theology.* Minneapolis: Fortress Press, 1992.

First Afrikan Presbyterian Church. *New Member Handbook.* Lithonia, Ga.: October 2002.

_____. "From the Pastor's Desk, Liturgical Calendar." *Talking Drums,* 1, no. 8. (October 2002).

Founder's Day Statement. Imani Temple Christian Fellowship, 2002.

Franklin, Robert, M. "The Safest Place on Earth: The Culture of Black Congregations." In *American Congregations, Volume 2: Perspectives in the Study of Congregations.* Ed. James P. Wind and James W. Lewis. Chicago: University of Chicago Press, 1994.

Gabriel, Stuart, and Joe P. Pattey. "Leaving Los Angeles: Migration, Economic Opportunity and Quality-of-Life." Southern California Studies Center. University of Southern California. http://www.frbsf.org/econrsrch/workingp/wp96-10.pdf.

Gallup, George Jr., and Timothy Jones. *The Next American Spirituality: Finding God in the 21st Century.* Colorado Springs: Victor/Cook Communications Ministry, 2000.

Gallup, George Jr., and Lindsay, D. Michael. *Surveying the Religious Landscape: Trends in U.S. Beliefs.* Harrisburg: Morehouse Publishing, 1999.

Gilkes, Cheryl Townsend. "'Plenty Good Room' . . . in a Changing Black Church." In *One Nation Under God?: Religion and American Culture*. Ed. Marjorie Garber and Rebecca L. Walkowitz. New York: Routledge, 1999.

_____ . "The Black Church as a Therapeutic Community: Areas of Suggested Research into the Black Religious Experience." *Journal of the Interdenominational Theological Center.* 8, 1 (1980): 29–44.

Grant, Jacquelyn. *White Women's Christ and Black Woman's Jesus: Feminist Christology and Womanist Response.* Atlanta: Scholars Press, 1989.

Gwynelle. *Practicing Kwanzaa Year Round: Affirmations and Activities Around the Seven Principles.* Summertown, Tenn.: Global Cultures, 2000.

Harding, Vincent. *Hope and Hisory: Why We Must Share the Story of the Movement.* New York: Orbis Books, 1990.

Harris, Forrest E. Sr., James T. Roberson, and Larry George, eds. *What Does It Mean to Be Black and Christian?: Pulpit, Pew, and Academy in Dialogue.* Nashville: Townsend Press, 1995.

Hayes, Diana. *Hagar's Daughters: Womanist Ways of Being in the World.* New York: Paulist Press, 1995.

Holt, Philip John, and Dominic A. Pacyga. *A Historical Guide to the Neighborhoods—The Loop and South Side.* Chicago: Chicago Historical Society, 1979.

Hopewell, James F. *Congregations: Stories and Structures.* Ed. Barbara Wheeler. Philadelphia: Fortress Press, 1987.

Hopkins, Dwight N. *Introducing Black Theology of Liberation.* New York: Orbis Books 1999.

"Is This New Wine?" Paper presented by African American Presbyterians for Prayer, Study and Action. August 22, 1993.

Jacobsen, Steve. *Heart to God, Hands to Work: Connecting Spiritually to Work.* Bethesda, Md.: Alban Institute, 1997.

Johnson, Stephanie Aisha Steplight. "Molefi K. Asante's Afrocentric Paradigm: A Model for Multiculturalism." In *Molefi Kete Asante and Afrocentricty: In Praise and in Criticism.* Ed. Dhyana Ziegler. Nashville: James C. Winston Publishing, 1995.

Karios Theologians (Group). *The Kairos Document, Challenge to the Churches: A Theological Comment on the Political Crisis in South Africa.* Grand Rapids, Mich.: W.B. Eerdman's, 1986.

Kaplan, Erin Aubry. "Ten Years and a Cloud of Dust: Crenshaw in Slow Motion." *LA Weekly,* April 26–May 2, 2002. http//www.laweekly.com /ink/02/03/the-kaplan.php.

Karenga, Maulana. *Introduction to Black Studies,* 2nd ed. Los Angeles: University of Sankore Press, 1993.

————. *Kwanzaa: A Celebration of Family, Community and Culture.* Los Angeles: University of Sankore Press, 1997.

Karenga, Maulana, and Jacob Carruthers, eds. *Kemet and the African Worldview: Research, Rescue and Restoration.* Los Angeles: University of Sankore Press, 1986.

Kilgore, Jini. *What Makes You So Strong? Sermons of Joy and Strength from Jeremiah A. Wright, Jr.* (Valley Forge, Pa.: Judson Press, 1993.

————. *Good News: Sermons of Hope for Today's Families.* Valley Forge, Pa.: Judson Press, 1995.

Kotey, Janette Elizabeth Chandler. *A Program to Raise the Faith Level in African-American Children Through Scripture, Kwanzaa Principles and Culture.* Doctoral dissertation (World Cat), 1999.

Lefkowitz, Mary. *Not Out of Africa: How Afrocentrism Became an Excuse to Teach Myth as History.* New York: Basic Books, 1996.

Lincoln, Eric C. *The Black Church Since Frazier.* New York: Schocken Books, 1974.

Los Angeles Metropolitan Churches Annual Report. "Prophetic Tradition in Action." Los Angeles: 2001/02.

Nascimento, Abdias do. *Africans in Brazil: A Pan-African Perspective.* Trenton, N.J.: Africa World Press, 1992.

Neimark, Phillip, and Justin M. Cordwell. *The Way of the Orisa: Empowering Your Life Through the Ancient African Religion of Ifa.* San Francisco: HarperCollins, 1993.

Paris, Peter. *The Spirituality of African Peoples: The Search for a Common Moral Discourse.* Minneapolis: Fortress Press, 1995.

————. *The Social Teachings of the Black Church.* Philadelphia: Fortress Press, 1988.

Pinn, Anthony. *The Black Church in the Post–Civil Rights Era.* New York: Orbis, 2002.

Pollard, Alton B. III. "The Civic Impact of the Black Church in Atlanta." In *The Status of Black Atlanta, 2002.* Atlanta: Southern Center for Studies in Public Policy, Clark Atlanta University, 2002.

Richards, Dona Maramba. *Let the Circle Be Unbroken: The Implications of African Spirituality in the Diaspora.* Trenton, N.J.: Red Sea Press, 1989.

Roberson, Erriel D. *The Maafa and Beyond: Remembrance, Ancestral Connections, and Nation Building for the African Global Community.* Columbia, Md.: Kugichagulia Press, 1995.

Roberts, Deotis, J. *Africentric Christianity: A Theological Appraisal for Ministry.* Valley Forge, Pa.: Judson Press, 2000.

Roof, Wade Clark. "Race and Residence in American Cities." *Annals of the American Academy of Political and Social Science,* Vol. 441 (January 1979).
_____. "Religion and Narrative." In *Review of Religious Research,* Vol. 34 No. 4, September, 1993.

Rooks, Charles Shelby. "Toward the Promised Land: An Analysis and the Religious Experience Black America." *The Black Church,* 2 (1973), 1–48.

Sanders, Cheryl, ed. *Living the Intersection: Womanism and Afrocentricism in Theology.* Minneapolis: Augsburg Fortress, 1995.

Seidman, Steven, ed. *The Postmodern Turn: New Perspectives on Social Theory.* Cambridge and New York: Cambridge University Press, 1994.

Sernet, Milton C. *Bound for the Promised Land: African American Religion and the Great Migration.* Durham, N.C.: Duke University Press, 1997.

Smith, Theophus, H. "The Spirituality of Afro-American Traditions." *Christian Spirituality: Post-Reformation and Modernity.* Ed. Louis Dupre, Don E. Saliers, and John Meyendorff. New York: Crossroads, 1989.

Stewart, Carlyle Fielding III. *Black Spirituality and Black Consciousness: Soul Force, Culture and Freedom in the African American Experience.* Trenton, N.J.: Africa World Press, 1999.

Sullivan, Maisha. "The Nguzo Saba: African-Centered Values as Tools for Family Assessment, Support and Empowerment." In *National Parent Information Network.* Virtual library. http://npin.org/library/2001/n00601.html.

Talmage, Franklin C. (prepared by Virginia [Mrs. Ben C.] Morris). *History of the Salem Presbyterian Church, Lithonia Georgia, DeKalb County, 1875–1953.*

Taylor, Quintard. "In Search of African American History in the West." *Smithsonian National Museum of African American History.* Behring Center, http://americanhistory.si.edu/paac/aquest/qtaylor.htm.

Thompson, Ernest Trice. *Presbyterians in the South, 1861–1890, Vol. II.* Richmond, Va.: John Knox Press, 1973.

T'Ofori-Atta, Ndugu. *ChristKwanzaa: An African American Church Liturgy, Derived from Traditional African Communal Celebration of the Harvest of the First Fruit: Matunda ya kwanza.* Clifton, N.Y.: Sturggler's Community Press, 1990.

Trinity United Church of Christ Annual Report. "Executive Council." Chicago: 1976.

Turner, Victor. *The Ritual Process.* New York: Cornell University Press, 1969.

Walker, Alice. *In Love and Trouble: Stories of Black Women.* San Diego, Harcourt Brace, 1973.

Weems, Renita. *Just A Sister Away: A Womanist Vision of Women's Relationships in the Bible*. Philadelphia: Innisfree Press, 1988.

Williams, Delores. *Sisters in the Wilderness: The Challenge of Womanist God-Talk*. Maryknoll, N.Y.: Orbis Books, 1993.

Wilmore, Gayraud S. "Identity and Integration: Black Presbyterians and Their Allies in the Twentieth Century." In *The Diversity of Discipleship: Presbyterianism and the 20th Century Christian Witness*. Ed. Milton J. Coalter, John M. Mulder, and Louis B. Weeks. Louisville: Westminster John Knox Press, 1991.

_____. *Black and Presbyterian: The Heritage and the Hope*. Louisville: Witherspoon Press, 1998.

_____. *Black Religion and Black Radicalism: An Interpretation of the Religious History of African Americans*. New York: Orbis Books, 1998.

Wind, James P., and James W. Lewis, eds. *American Congregations, Volume 2: New Perspectives in the Study of Congregations*. Chicago: University of Chicago, 1994.

Wuthnow, Robert. *After Heaven: Spirituality in America Since the 1950s*. Los Angeles: University of California Press, 1998.

Index